The Grief Walk

Losing, Grieving, and Journeying on to Something New

Alister G. Hendery

Philip Garside Publishing Ltd.

Copyright © 2020 Alister Graeme Hendery

This book or any portion thereof may not be reproduced or used in any manner whatsoever without the express written permission of the publisher except for the use of brief quotations in a book review.

Unless otherwise indicated, Scripture quotations are from the *New Revised Standard Version Bible*: Anglicised Edition, copyright © 1989, 1995, Division of Christian Education of the National Council of the Churches of Christ in the United States of America. Used by permission. All rights reserved.

Quotations marked *NLT* are taken from the *Holy Bible*, New Living Translation, copyright © 1996, 2004, 2015 by Tyndale House Foundation. Used by permission of Tyndale House Publishers, Inc., Carol Stream, Illinois 60188. All rights reserved.

Quotations marked *ANZPB* are taken from *A New Zealand Prayer Book, He Karakia Mihinare o Aotearoa*. Copyright © is held by the Anglican Church in Aotearoa, New Zealand and Polynesia. Used by permission. All rights reserved. Available at: http://anglicanprayerbook.nz/

Poems from Hilary Smith, *Grief's Shadowed Path: Poems of Loss and Healing* (Napier: EVBooks, 2017), are used with permission.

Also by Alister Hendery:

Earthed in Hope: Dying, Death and Funerals – A Pākehā Anglican Perspective (Wellington: Philip Garside Publishing Ltd., 2014)

Note to Readers:
Some names and identifying details have been changed, and some people portrayed are composites.

International Print edition
ISBN 978-1-98-857241-3

Philip Garside Publishing Ltd
PO Box 17160
Wellington 6147
New Zealand

bookspgpl@gmail.com — www.pgpl.co.nz
PDF, ePub and Kindle editions also available

Cover photograph: Alexander Garside—Garside Imaging
Author photograph: Simon Hendery

Contents

Foreword 7
Preface 9
Acknowledgements 11
How I use certain Words 12
Authors who have Influenced Me 13
1 – Introduction 15
2 – Our Lives are Laden with Losses 19
    Acknowledging our Losses 22
    Disenfranchised Losses and Griefs 24
3 – Experiences of Disenfranchised Loss and Grief 28
    Grieving for Those Still Living 29
    Living Loss and Disability 31
    Relational Loss – Divorce and Dissolution 35
    Relational Loss – Ending of a Romantic Relationship 38
    Unrecognised Relationships 39
    The Loss of a Companion Animal 41
    Material Losses 44
    Infertility and Childlessness 47
    Grief in Foster Care 51
    The Losses of Miscarriage and Stillbirth 54
    Loss from Medical Termination 56
    Loss of Employment 58
    Loss through Abuse 59
    Discovering Disenfranchisement 60
    Change and Transition 62
4 – Understandings and Misunderstandings about Grief ... 65
    Our Loss and Grief is Unique – so Forget the Rules 65
    There's No 'One Size Fits All' – so Forget Stages in Grief ... 67
    We Wax and Wane – so it's Okay to Retreat
    from Time to Time 70

    A Continual Presence Which can Ambush us
    – so Forget the Timeline 72
    Continuing Bonds – So Forget about Having to Let Go 75
    Grief Doesn't get Closed Off – so Forget about Closure.............77
    Our Life has Changed – so Forget the idea of
    Returning to Normal 79
    We Grieve in Our Own Way – so Forget the Stereotypes 80

5 – Experiencing Grief 84
    More than Sadness 84
    Grief Isolates 86
    Experiencing Grief in our Body 89
    Experiencing Grief in our Emotions 91
    Experiencing Grief in our Thinking and Mental processes 95
    Experiencing Grief in our Behaviour 97
    Experiencing Grief in our Spirituality 99
    Secondary Losses and Loss of Identity 101
    When do we Need Professional Interventions? 104

6 – What do I say? What can I do? 107
    Sit Beside me on my Mourning Bench 107
    Some Dos and Don'ts 111
    Do Talk About the Loss 113
    It's about Relationships 117
    Caring Companionship 118
    Silence, Tears, and Empathy 120

7 – Grief is about Love and Attachment 123
    Grief – the Price of Love 123
    Love as Attachment 124
    A Secure Base 126

8 – God and our Grief – But what Kind of God? 129
    Our Vulnerable God 129
    Good News Stories of Vulnerability, Loss, and Grief 130
    Becoming Vulnerable – Becoming like God 134
    Suffering Love that is *With* Us 134

Discarding the Great Vacuum Cleaner in the Sky 138
Jesus Began to Weep 141

9 – Words for our Grief – A Gift from the Psalms 144
David's Dirge 145
Faith Incorporating Grief 151
My One Companion is Darkness 155
Challenging a Cover-up 158

10 – Walking with Job – A Story of Losing and Grieving 163
The Scene is Set – Job 1:1 – 2:10 163
Job's Friends – Job 2:11–13 164
What the Friends got Right 164
Sitting Shiva 165
What the Friends got Wrong 167
Job's Wife 170
What Job Needed – Giving Voice to his Grief 171
Anger and the Need to Blame 172
Job's Questioning 173
Faith Containing Tensions 176
The Climax – Job 38–41 177
Our Faith may be Challenged and Changed 178

11 – The Easter Walk 180
Waiting in the Darkness and the Absence 180
Gradual, Imperceptible Resurrection 183

12 – A Choice – Do we go Through the Pain or Around it? 186
Stewards of our Pain 187
A Great Freedom – How do we Respond? 192

13 – Our Search for Meaning after Loss 194
Moving Grief from a Noun to a Verb 194
What is Meaning? 194
Reconstructing our Meaning after Loss 195
Meaning in Love 198
Living in a Changed World 200

14 – Hope Emerges **205**
    Hopes and Goals 205
    Hope Isn't a Magic Potion...206
    Our Sustaining Hope: If God is for us.....................................208

Selected Bibliography **211**

Index **213**
    Also by Alister G. Hendery
    from Philip Garside Publishing Ltd..216

Foreword

This book isn't long. Not many pages.

But this book takes a lifetime of pain, fear, disappointment, struggle, and elation. It's a book that will read you as you are reading it. It is a book you will pick up and put down and pick up and put down as you find yourself walking again through parts of your life, maybe unexpectedly rediscovering boggy patches you had forgotten, or not realised are still painful.

You will relive many things through Alister's words. Because within these pages are the revealing reflections of many people. Some have written books. Others have shared their experiences with Alister in informal ways. There is ancient wisdom here alongside modern psychology. There is gentleness, and there is a reality faced that grief is universal, painful, and not always an easy walk. There is the important forth-telling that grief is about more experiences than the physical death of one we love. And that everyone carries grief about many losses in our life. Everyone.

You will find practical knowledge here too. Ways to be kind and compassionate with each other. Challenges to reconsider some of our responses to each other. Words to not say. Silences to keep. Compassion to spring from our own life's griefs as we encounter those deep places in others. Trust to build by being 'alone together' as Arnold Lobel puts it in *Frog and Toad Together*.

If grief is that universal alone experience, Alister reminds us that the walk through that dark valley builds us as it challenges us. Learning to allow ourselves to identify what we're feeling, experiencing, and fearing is hard because so much of grief is not encouraged to be shared. Finding another who is alongside us is a gift. Allowing ourselves to be alongside others is also a gift. This book opens that door in deceptively simple ways.

The Grief Walk

I can envisage myself offering this book as a group reading, a Lenten study, a winter series perhaps. I will certainly offer it to folk to read by themselves too.

But beware. As I read Alister's words I found myself thinking, lamenting, crying, and laughing. I found myself walking quietly round the lake. I surprised myself with the depth of some of what rose to the surface for me. Ancient griefs, recent disappointments, and the ambivalent feelings that came, like fish to breathe the air again.

I found myself dwelling on the ancient wisdom of Isaiah: 'He was a man of sorrows, and acquainted with grief: and we hid as it were our faces from him; he was despised, and we esteemed him not' (Isaiah 53:3). For many people this is their experience too – faces hidden, folk not able to manage someone else's grief. As this book reads you, may it also encourage you to be with others differently.

I came to value the reflection that arrived unbidden as I read this book. I have learned more about myself through reading it. For that I am grateful.

The Rev'd Rob Ferguson

Preface

I met Isabel a few years after her husband John died. As she shared her experience of grief, I asked her what she needed most from others in the aftermath of John's death when she felt abandoned and alone. Her response was immediate. 'Someone who would walk with me. Not people who would talk at me and give me answers, but simply listen to me and walk with me.' Isabel and I coined the phrase, *the grief walk*. As our conversations continued, we realised that this walk is also about the journey we take as we embrace our grief and seek a new life after our loss.

Those conversations are reflected in this book, which I offer as a resource as we explore how we can walk with others in their grief and how we might respond to our own experiences of loss. The most valuable gift that we can give a person in grief is the gift of our presence and companionship. We don't give advice or solutions because we all differ in the ways we experience and express grief. We walk with them, listening and accepting their pain.

Isabel told me, 'In the first months of my grief walk, so many obstacles strewed my path to a new life – a continued living. Looking back I see how I had no energy or will to move forward. I still find myself falling into this way of thinking and have to stop and evaluate.' That's how it is for many of us. Grief is a tough and chaotic experience that may last a lifetime. Knowing this doesn't lessen the pain but it reminds us that we are normal.

Sometimes all we can do in grief is, as Isabel put it, continue living, putting one foot in front of the other. Then, in time, our grief walk may take small, tentative turns as we begin to discover new life. Many resources on grief focus on typical reactions we may experience after a loss. That's important, but they stop at that point. I don't. I go on to explore how we can continue the grief walk and live creatively in a world that's been radically changed. When we befriend our grief and allow ourselves to experience the pain we continue the journey to something new.

The Grief Walk

Loss and grief have been a special focus of my ministry for the past 40 years. It's a ministry that's included work as a counsellor and funeral celebrant, a pastor with a particular care for the dying and the bereaved, and as a transitional priest, ministering with faith communities in times of change and loss. Reflecting on those years of ministry, as well as my own experiences of loss and grief, it struck me that many of the losses we experience aren't acknowledged.

Much of what is written about grief focuses on our reactions to the death of a loved one. This is probably the toughest experience of loss that most of us face and it may well be the reason you picked up this book. It's not, however, the only form of loss we encounter. Our lives are marked by countless other losses, many of which we don't recognise or others don't acknowledge. We may grieve these unacknowledged losses in silence, receiving little or no support and understanding. I explore some of these unacknowledged losses and illustrate them with stories shared with me from many different people. While each experience is utterly unique, they show there's a universal dimension. We aren't alone in our grieving.

Psychology deeply influences our understanding of grief. I respect what psychology can teach us, and throughout this book I draw on contemporary psychological insights. It's not, however, the only lens through which we can view loss and grief. Christian spirituality also has a special gift to offer us in our understanding of the grief walk as we seek to find new meaning in our lives after a loss. I've written this book from that viewpoint, as I believe God who is Love grieves with us and is the source of something new.

A free **Reflective Study Guide** for *The Grief Walk*
is available to download on the publisher's website here:

https://pgpl.co.nz/study-guide-for-the-grief-walk/

Acknowledgements

In writing this book I've drawn on the wisdom of many people, and I'm indebted to those who gave me permission to include their experiences. Their stories are a treasured gift. My own experiences are also etched in these pages. I gratefully acknowledge those who have walked with me during my own seasons of loss and grief.

A number of people reviewed sections of my work. I owe a special debt of gratitude to Susan Haldane, Hilary Smith, Helen and Bosco Peters, David Earle, Kitty Broome, and Deborah Broome. Thank you to Katie Boyle for her insights and proofing skills. None of those who reviewed my work and offered their advice are responsible for the views I express. These are, of course, mine alone. I owe Hilary Smith additional thanks for allowing me to quote her poems. Her writing is borne out of her own stories of loss. Hilary's words are straightforward, yet they express the complexity of grief: the inner chaos, the contradictions, tensions and struggles that we experience in the wake of a loss. I am grateful to Deborah Broome for her substantial contribution to chapter 10 – 'Walking with Job.' This chapter is based on a paper that Deborah and I co-authored. Then there is my publisher, Philip Garside. My thanks to Philip for his patience, understanding, and encouragement.

The circles of love that encompass our lives keep us going through the tough times. They are a gift from the One who is Love. They sustain and nurture us through their presence and companionship. It's to those who encircle my life with love that I dedicate this book – especially my wife Deborah.

How I use certain Words

I dislike euphemisms. We use them to avoid reality. For instance, phrases like 'passed away' or 'passed' are part of the denial of death that permeates Western culture. Many Christians have bought into this unhelpful dynamic. How ridiculous it would be to say that Jesus passed away on the cross. A parishioner, whose son had died, brought home to me the absurdity of euphemisms. 'When people talk about me losing my son, it makes me sound so careless. I haven't mislaid my son. He's dead. I know exactly where he is.' I would like to explain how I have chosen to use certain words.

The terms *loss, grief, bereavement,* and *mourning* are frequently used interchangeably. I use them in the following ways.

Bereavement: The ancient roots of the word can mean to be deprived, robbed, plundered, or despoiled. I use *bereavement* to refer to the state or experience of deprivation or loss as a result of physical death.

Loss: I use this word to refer to the loss of anything or anyone by any means. In everyday life I don't refer to the death of someone by this word. However, because this book refers to all and any losses we may experience, I employ the word *loss* inclusively, though it's interchangeable with *bereavement* and contains the experience of being deprived, plundered, robbed, or despoiled.

Grief: There are two elements in how I use this word. First, it refers to our personal *reactions* to a loss. Second, it speaks about how we choose to *respond* to our loss.

Mourning: This word is used in various ways though it's often synonymous with grief. It can also be used to refer to societal or cultural expressions of bereavement behaviour and practices, which is how I generally use it.

Authors who have Influenced Me

Three authors in particular have influenced me.

Clive Staples Lewis (commonly referred to as C. S. Lewis) was a notable Christian thinker of the last century. In 1956, at the age of 57, C. S. Lewis married Joy Davidman, and just four years later Joy died of cancer. Her death and the intensity of his grief plunged C. S. Lewis into a crisis of faith. Following Joy's death he wrote a chronicle of his grief, which he described as a kind of 'map of sorrow,' a 'safety valve' to prevent a 'total collapse.' C. S. Lewis never intended this personal journal be published. When he finally permitted *A Grief Observed*[1] to be printed, it was under a pen name. Not until after his death was the work identified as Lewis'.

A Grief Observed is an extraordinary reflection on one person's struggle with the vagaries of loss and grief and, in particular, his struggles with and about God. This chronicle doesn't supply neat religious answers. Far from it. It offers a deeply honest examination of the grief experience and the journey to hard-won hope.

Nicholas Wolterstorff is a professor of philosophical theology. In 1983 his 24-year-old son Eric died in a mountain climbing accident in Austria. Over the following year Nicholas wrote his reflections on his grief. Published as *Lament for a Son*, this work reveals Nicholas' wrestling with the reality of death and suffering, the presence and absence of God, and the challenges that these struggles raise for a person of faith. He also recognises that in grief's 'particularity there is universality' and that what he shares gives voice to 'the pain of many forms of loss.'[2]

Both these works are loaded with questions as these two men seek, in quite different ways, to make sense of the loss that has been inflicted on them. I have found that questions can be more valuable than

---

1 C. S. Lewis, *A Grief Observed* (London: Faber and Faber, 1961).
2 Nicholas Wolterstorff, *Lament for a Son* (Grand Rapids, Michigan: Wm. B Eerdmans Publishing Co., 1987), 5.

answers. Questions drive us to seek meaning that is true for us. They keep our faith awake and moving; they sustain us on our journey.

Viktor Frankl, a psychiatrist and psychotherapist, was an Austrian Jew sent to a Nazi concentration camp. He survived the Holocaust and published *Man's Search for Meaning* in 1946.[3] This book is about what enabled him and others to survive. I was drawn to this work by his insight that we cannot control many things that happen to us in life, but we can always control how we choose to respond, and that the primary purpose of life is the quest for meaning.

---

3   Viktor E. Frankl, *Man's Search for Meaning* (Boston: Beacon Press, 2014).

1 – Introduction

'For everything there is a season… A time to cry and a time to laugh. A time to grieve and a time to dance' (Ecclesiastes 3:1a, 4 *NLT*). The Hebrew sage is right, for grief is integral to our lives.

We grieve when we lose someone or something that matters to us. Because our existence is punctuated with innumerable losses, grief permeates our lives. Grieving is as natural as sleeping when we are tired and eating when we are hungry. Yet, for many of us, grief is alien. We push it away and think that in time it will disappear. That's probably what we hope for when we talk about 'moving on' and finding some mythical state called 'closure'. The problem is, our grief doesn't evaporate. It hangs around waiting for acknowledgement, waiting for us to respond to it.

Working on this book reminded me at a personal level how grief seeps into the crevices of our lives. Absorbed in research I would unexpectedly find myself immersed in an old grief or facing a loss that I had never acknowledged. We carry our grief deep within. That's why it can ambush us. We attend the funeral of someone who we were not greatly attached to and find ourselves undergoing a jumble of inconsolable emotions. We watch a movie and suddenly we are crying our eyes out. It has nothing to do with what's happening on the screen, but it has triggered a loss experience that may be decades old. Grief's path can't be predicted. Grief goes where it chooses and takes the time it needs. As you read on, don't be surprised if you find yourself facing an unidentified grief or one that you thought you had disposed of.

Grief denied or ignored can fester and affect our well-being. It can consume us as grief is laid upon grief. Our culture doesn't help us. We create a grief box in which we confine the grieving person and wait for them to emerge fixed and whole again. The grief box comes with expectations that range from the time we are allowed to grieve to the emotions we are permitted and expected to express. It's a stifling container. Those of us who have been confined to it know how it's easier, when asked how we are, to simply smile and say, 'Not too bad' or 'Fine thanks.' That's far safer than revealing our pain and vulnerability, because if we do, we may well be informed, 'You should be over it by now.' … 'Focus on the positives.' … 'Trust in God.' … 'Others are worse off than you.' Consequently, we have learned to hide our grief. If we reveal it, we risk judgment and hurtful clichés. It's my hope that you may discover within yourself permission to honour your losses and help others find the freedom to be honest about theirs.

While grief is our natural response to loss, sometimes it can be overwhelming and devastating. Our understanding of loss and grief must be able to match the realities that we experience and not be subject to some theoretical model that's held up as 'the right way' to grieve. So also our relationship with God. We need a spirituality that's capable of embracing experiences that may rock our trust in God and throw into disarray all that previously made sense of life.

I experience grief as like a journey. Although others have traversed this terrain, it's a journey unique to each of us. For this reason, there's no definitive roadmap for the grief walk, though there are signposts: indicators that can guide us as we walk (or, as it will often feel, stagger) down this path. I intend this book as a guide on this walk; not a roadmap, but a description of what you might find on your grief walk and how you might help others negotiate theirs.

I explore typical reactions we often experience after a loss. There are also misunderstandings that can inhibit us coping with loss and prevent us from moving towards something new. It's not enough to just talk about our reactions to loss. We need to go further and look at how we can live in a world that has been radically changed and find new hope and meaning after our loss. Treat what I offer as suggestions; insights I've gained on my journey that may or may not resonate with you.

You will not find in this book a ready-made formula for overcoming grief, because I don't believe it's something we overcome. Though grief need not overcome us, and though after a season we can adapt to a new reality and even be transformed by the experience, the

Introduction

loss remains a part of us. It's something we learn to encompass. I've discovered that when, instead of stifling my grief, I honour it, I don't become despondent and depressed. On the contrary, after a time I grow more hopeful. This doesn't eradicate the pain, but I've found that we can begin a journey on which loss and grief enriches the tapestry of our lives. Embracing our grief, rather than treating it as an unwelcome intruder, allows us to choose how we respond, and that's empowering.

Western culture exalts individualism and self-reliance. We have learned to grieve alone and to keep our pain to ourselves. I suggest another approach; one rooted in the conviction that we find meaning in relationship. We ought to be able to share, with both God and members of our community of faith, the pain of our grief. I'm conscious that some faith communities are not gatherings where we can be honest about our grief. In these the only sounds that are sanctioned are those of praise and victory. Christians are, however, the inheritors of a spirituality that says we may also rant and rave at God, pour out our sorrow and pain, question and doubt the divine. As we do this together, we discover hope.

I'm aware that for many the church is the very cause of their loss and grief. As a pastor I know this only too well, and some of my own losses and hurts have their roots in church life. Yet it's from within the community of faith, flawed and frail though we all are, that I've learned what it is to be loved as well as to love, and to be healed as well as being an agent of healing. A faith community doesn't just exist for itself. In my tradition we are sent out at the end of every service of worship with the words, 'Go now to love and serve the Lord. Go in peace.' We reply, 'Amen. We go in the name of Christ.'[4] Integral to this going, loving, serving, and sharing peace is to be with those who grieve; to be with those who are broken by suffering. Sometimes the person I'm called to be with is myself. I can only walk with you in your grief if I'm willing and able to recognise and live with my own griefs. Through the reflections and narratives offered in this book, I aim to provide you with a resource to help you do the same.

---

4   *A New Zealand Prayer Book, He Karakia Mihinare o Aotearoa*, 429.

The Grief Walk

As you read this book I suggest you keep three things in mind. First, I'm very aware that at times it may be best to imitate Job and 'cover my mouth with my hand' for I may 'have said too much already' (Job 40:3-5 *NLT*). In the presence of suffering and pain, silence is sometimes the most appropriate response. As you read on you will find yourself reflecting on your experiences of grief. I encourage you to take the time to lay my words aside and be with your experience. It's only when we allow ourselves to experience our pain that our grief walk can take us to something new.

Second, the short narratives I share remind us that grief is first and foremost the cry of a wounded and broken heart. The story of loss and grief that matters most of all is not mine, nor that of others, but yours. Honour your story. As you read through this book you may find it helpful to keep notes or a journal. You may also find it appropriate to share and explore your reflections, questions, and experiences with a trusted friend or spiritual companion.

Third, in my earlier book, *Earthed in Hope: Dying, Death and Funerals,* I ended the Introduction with these words: 'If we do not lead people to the love of God, where is the hope of which Scripture speaks?'[5] I begin this book with the same question.

---

5 Alister G. Hendery, *Earthed in Hope: Dying, Death and Funerals – A Pākehā Anglican Perspective* (Wellington: Philip Garside Publishing Ltd., 2014), 14.

2 – Our Lives are Laden with Losses

We experience loss and grief far more often than we realise. Even if no one close to us has died, we know about loss and we grieve, though we may not describe the experience in those terms.

> Loss and grief meet us in simple phrases spoken to us and by us.
>
> We're moving.
> I'm leaving you.
> We don't need you anymore.
> You're redundant.
> It's cancer.
> It's a disability that you'll have to learn to live with.
> You'll need a mastectomy.
> I recommend that we put your pet down.
> Your building is an earthquake risk.
> I'm going overseas to study.
> I can't trust you anymore.
> It's not possible for you to have birth children.

Common to all experiences of loss is knowing that our life has been changed; we must now face a new reality. Life as it was, no longer exists. The death of a loved one can be the most intense form of loss that most of us will experience. It's irrevocable. Nicholas Wolterstorff describes it poignantly.

> It is the *neverness* that is so painful. *Never again* to be here with us – never to sit with us at table, never to travel with us, never to laugh with us, never to cry with us, never to embrace us as he leaves for school, never to see his brothers and sisters marry. All the rest of our lives we must live without him. Only our death can stop the pain of his death.[6]

---

[6] Wolterstorff, *Lament for a Son*, 15.

The Grief Walk

The neverness is the sting of grief, be it the loss of a person through death or some other form of loss. What causes such pain is the knowledge that someone, some place, some thing, some part of us shall never be again. The future that we planned or hoped for has gone. Our personal world that was so familiar to us has been taken away.

Our lives are laden with endings and farewells, losses and deaths, separations and partings. When that happens, grief is not far behind. While no catalogue of losses can ever be complete, consider those listed below and note those that resonate with you and ones that you would add. As you identify your losses, simply acknowledge them and honour their presence in your life. Do not judge or compare them.

- Loss of good health
- Loss of part of our physical body
- Loss of self-respect or dignity
- Loss of identity – I'm not the person I used to be
- Loss of reputation or social standing
- Loss of an opportunity
- Loss of hopes and dreams for the future
- Loss of how things were
- Loss of material possessions
- Loss of financial stability
- Loss of lifestyle
- Loss of a sense of safety
- Loss of innocence
- Loss of independence
- Loss of language, culture, and tradition
- Loss of faith or religious identity
- Loss of a pet
- Loss through adoption

- Loss through foster care
- Infertility
- Wanting a child but not having a partner with whom to have a child
- Miscarriage
- Medical termination
- Failure
- Ending of a relationship
- Estrangement from family
- Feeling abandoned by a parent who is involved in a divorce or separation
- Farewell to friends
- Moving to a new house and leaving a familiar place
- A child leaving home
- A partner or spouse moving into care
- Retirement
- Work redundancy
- Loss of financial security
- The ending of a responsibility that we've held
- The discovery that someone wasn't who we thought they were
- Loss of the person we knew through Alzheimer's or dementia
- Loss of the person we knew through mental illness
- Loss of the person we knew through a traumatic injury
- Loss of a person through incarceration
- Loss of a person who died before we were born

Some days it may seem that no sooner do we feel that we have come to terms with one loss than another comes along and disrupts our familiar patterns.

The Grief Walk

In the following sections I talk about recognising losses that might not be considered losses and explain some reasons we don't regard them as something to grieve.

Acknowledging our Losses

In order to grieve we need to name and recognise our losses. Why is this important? Grief associated with the death of a loved one is something others readily affirm as a normal reaction, but the grief that accompanies many other losses goes unrecognised and unacknowledged. These losses and griefs are not ones that we normally identify as such. We may think of them as stresses or difficulties in adjustment, and so we minimise them. 'It's no big deal. It was just a job. I'll make new friends. New opportunities will emerge. Toughen up, pull yourself together, and move on.' But then we find ourselves struggling to pull ourselves together, struggling to move on. We wonder why we cannot just get on with life as it was before the loss. And, if we do recognise the loss as something significant, we are tempted to bury it. The trouble is, losses we don't appropriately acknowledge result in our grief remaining buried deep within ourselves, and, in time, can wreak havoc: emotionally, physically, relationally, behaviourally, and spiritually. Our forebears recognised this. In the 17th century, one of the listed causes of death was grief. We still talk of dying of a broken heart, recognising the physical and emotional strain.

Jan had a special relationship with her Grandad. All through her early years Grandad lived in the same house, becoming Jan's constant companion and best friend. When she was 16, he died.

> 'I didn't see him after he died, and his funeral was a sombre and bleak affair. My family didn't discuss what had happened and I was told not to cry, as it would upset others. So I didn't cry. I pushed my sadness so far down that it wouldn't come out. I got very sick with throat and mouth ulcers.
>
> Fast forward some years... Visiting a bookshop I came across *Gramp*[7] – a moving photographic record of a grandfather's

---
7   Mark Jury and Dan Jury, *Gramp* (Harmondsworth, Middlesex: Penguin Books, 1976).

death. I would visit the bookshop and look at *Gramp*. I could only ever look at a page or two at a time before I would start to cry. Eventually I bought the book and read it right through. It was what I needed to unblock my long-suppressed sadness and acknowledge how much I missed my Grandad.'

Over the years Jan learned not to be afraid of her grief, not to bottle it up, though she acknowledges that this can be hard.

'To express it when it surfaces, is like releasing pressure. Once emotions are shut down, they are hard to unlock. It can cause illness and depression, but it's scary to contemplate unleashing them.'

Grief is powerful, as the Roman poet Ovid knew. 'Suppressed grief suffocates, it rages within the breast, and is forced to multiply its strength.' However much we seek to push grief away, it will demand our attention – and it will get it one way or another.

When grief lies unacknowledged because we fail to recognise it as grief, we may interpret and respond to the loss in ways that are unhelpful or inappropriate. When we do know it is grief, but we choose to ignore it, the consequences are, as Jan observed, detrimental. It's well understood and accepted that our physical health is related to our emotional health. The physical body is affected by negative psychological stress.

Grieving is the process by which we adjust to living with a loss. Until we name and acknowledge a loss, we are unable to reconcile ourselves to it. We cannot reconstruct our lives without the person or thing that we have lost until we have recognised the loss. To put it another way, we cannot treat a wound if we do not know what or where the wound is.

We tend to compare losses, thinking that one loss is harder than another. 'She had a good innings – she made it to 90.' 'People have been through far worse.' The implication being, certain types of loss are less worthy of grief, less deserving of support and attention than others. It's a judgement we make on ourselves.

> David had been made redundant. He worked for the company for over 30 years, and because of his age, he knew he would struggle to get another position. As he expressed his hurt and fears, tears came to his eyes. Then he suddenly stopped. 'But what I'm going through is nothing. I mustn't complain. One of my mates has got terminal cancer. I've got to stop feeling sorry for myself. My loss is nothing compared to what he's facing.'

David's loss *does* matter, and it *is* something. Every loss creates its own issues. Each hurts in its own unique way. The loss that matters and needs to be recognised and honoured is the one that we are dealing with right now.

Disenfranchised Losses and Griefs

When, for whatever reason, we are denied the right to grieve and our loss isn't recognised, it's called disenfranchised grief. Kenneth Doka, who undertook ground-breaking work in this area, writes, 'Disenfranchised losses are not openly acknowledged, socially sanctioned, or publicly shared. They create a paradox. We experience loss, but we come to believe we do not have the right to grieve that loss.'[8] Disenfranchisement occurs when our loss and grief isn't validated. This may occur for several reasons.

People don't recognise it as a loss and don't sanction the grief. Andrea found this after experiencing, in the space of a year, a miscarriage and a divorce.

> No one said to me 'You aren't allowed to grieve these losses,' but their actions and words showed that I should keep my grief to myself. I was subtly, and not so subtly told, that I had to move on. So I learned that when asked how I was, to reply, 'Fine thanks.' That's what people expected of me, and I came to expect it of myself. But I couldn't move on. I ended up stuck in a loop, wondering why I couldn't escape – why my grief was all-consuming.

---

8   Kenneth J. Doka, *Grief is a Journey: Finding your Path through Loss* (New York: Atria Books, 2016), 184.

People either don't appreciate or understand our relationship to the person we have lost. Society defines who we are allowed to grieve. It sets 'grieving rules' and these have even been codified in legislation. Under New Zealand law an employee who has been in a position for six months is entitled to three day's bereavement leave when a member of the 'immediate family' dies. One day's bereavement leave *may* be granted, at the employer's discretion, on the death of a person outside the immediate family. In other words, if the death falls outside this definition, we don't have a socially sanctioned right to grieve.[9]

Societal rules exclude not only losses that don't involve the death of an immediate family member but also disregard bereavement because our relationship with the person who has died isn't recognised, for example, the death of a:

- former partner or spouse
- work colleague
- online friend
- same-gender partner or spouse (under New Zealand law this relationship is recognised but some religious traditions reject it)
- friend, neighbour, or acquaintance
- sibling, especially an adult sibling
- distant relation
- foster parent or child
- step-parent or step-child

---

9   As I write the New Zealand Parliament is considering a bill that will 'make it clear that an unplanned end of a pregnancy by miscarriage or still-birth constitutes grounds for bereavement leave for the mother and her partner or spouse.' 'Holidays (Bereavement Leave for Miscarriage) Amendment Bill (No 2).' Accessed from https://www.parliament.nz/en/pb/bills-and-laws/bills-proposed-laws/document/BILL_89457/holidays-bereavement-leave-for-miscarriage-amendment

- partner in an extramarital relationship
- caregiver, nurse, pastor, counsellor, or other 'professional' relationship of care.

The way a person dies may be considered unworthy of grief. This happens when someone kills themselves, dies from a drug overdose, or dies as a result of criminal activity.

Disenfranchisement can extend to the way we grieve. People might not acknowledge our grief in the absence of outward expression of emotion, or, they may consider our expression of grief 'over the top.' This is reflected in statements like, 'You should be over it by now.' … 'It's time to move on.' … 'It's not as if she was your wife.' … 'You only saw him occasionally.'

The person grieving may be considered not capable of grieving. Despite over-whelming evidence to the contrary, both the very old and very young are often seen by others as having little comprehension of or reaction to the death of a significant person in their life. Similarly, mentally disabled persons may also be disenfranchised in grief.

Then there's self-disenfranchisement. We disenfranchise ourselves because we, the griever, don't acknowledge our grief, or we believe that we should not be grieving. This is normally because of a sense of shame. 'I feel so embarrassed over my grief at the death of my pet.' It can also extend to our feelings. 'I shouldn't be feeling like this.'

When disenfranchisement occurs, for whatever reason, we find ourselves isolated and alone in our pain. We tend to think that our responses are all wrong and inappropriate, so we feel unable to talk about them, unable to express them, unable to seek support. We bear our grief in silence, and the silence compounds the grief. Silence leaves us unsupported by our community, friends, and family, and our loss goes unacknowledged. Because we often grieve in silence, we don't recognise that we are grieving. We don't understand the true cause of the reactions we are experiencing, thinking we are being silly or over sensitive, or perhaps attributing our reactions to some other cause.

Some people experience losses and griefs that fall into these categories and don't experience disenfranchisement, and that's good. Not only are they able to name their loss but they are also able to receive supportive acknowledgement for the depth of their loss from others, even in a situation that is commonly disenfranchised. What I know is that for many this isn't the case. I posed a public question on Facebook, seeking people's experiences of disenfranchised loss and grief. Many people responded quickly. For a number of people, it was the first time they had been given the opportunity to name their loss and for their grief to be recognised. As Melissa Kelly, who teaches pastoral care and counselling writes, 'All losses are not created equal. We pay more attention to some losses than to others. And some losses never make it onto our radar screen at all.'[10]

---

10   Melissa M. Kelley, *Grief: Contemporary Theory and the Practice of Ministry* (Minneapolis: Fortress Press, 2010), 11.

3 – Experiences of Disenfranchised Loss and Grief

I spent time with two women who, in quite different ways, were experiencing profound grief. Their losses are major, but they aren't recognised and acknowledged as losses. Both women are experiencing disenfranchised grief.

> Jo is in her mid 80s. She's left her house in which she has lived for over 40 years, and because of failing health, has moved into a rest home. When family members visit, she complains about her small room, the institutional food, her inability to go and make cheese on toast in the middle of the night, and the absence of familiar belongings. Jo's family is getting impatient with her complaining. What they don't recognise is her grief. Her losses are multiple. As well as the loss of good health, Jo is experiencing the loss of independence, the loss of possessions, her sense of usefulness to others, and the loss of a home that contained untold memories.

> Anna, who is now in her early 30s, gave birth to her son and daughter when she was a teenager. She describes her losses. 'I cry with the grief of having not been able to celebrate like other couples do – not having people excited for me like other expectant mothers when they announce their pregnancies – missing out on having a partner to share it all with – for the loss of my youth – the loss of social normality, and time to explore who I really was. These losses from the past can still come and hit me hard like it was yesterday.'

Disenfranchised grief isn't black-or-white; it's a relative and subjective experience. You and I may experience a similar type of loss and in your cultural, social, or religious situation the loss is 'openly acknowledged, socially sanctioned or publicly mourned' (to use Kenneth Doka's phrase), whereas in mine, it isn't. Experiences of disenfranchised loss and grief differ dramatically from person to person and community to community. The examples I offer need to be read with that in mind. I also share these stories so that, as one contributor wrote, 'others may know that in the pain that feels so solitary and goes unacknowledged, they may know they aren't alone.'

By acknowledging these losses, we recognise the grief they generate. We can't change overnight our social and communal norms around loss and grief, but we can take control of how we respond. This is critical, for even if our grief is disenfranchised, it's by acknowledging it, by recognising a loss to be a loss that we grant ourselves the freedom to grieve and the opportunity to grow from our loss.

Grieving for Those Still Living

The pain of losing a family member or a friend before they physically die can be very raw and isolating. A daughter, whose mother suffers from advanced dementia, describes the pain she experiences.

> I feel like no one understands the pain and grief I feel as I watch my mother living with dementia. If I try and talk about it, people quickly shut me down, and tell me I should be happy that she's still alive. But sometimes it hurts so much that I wish she were physically dead.

The son of a parent with Alzheimer's expressed his experience this way.

> Mum lived the last 15 years of her life with Alzheimer's disease. As her illness advanced people told me that they chose not to visit her because, 'We wish to remember her as she was.' The woman they knew no longer existed. That was true – too true – though I wonder if their decision not to visit was also a fear of facing the pain of their grief. For myself, the roles had reversed. I now fed, comforted, and held like a toddler, the woman who had given birth to me – who had nurtured and loved me, fed me, and changed my nappies. The mother I had known for 45 years no longer existed. It was a living death. I grieved deeply – but I grieved silently. Few people shared my ongoing grief. Most chose to stay away. Years after her death I realised I had lost many of my memories of my mother. The last season of her life swamped the former decades. I now ask others to tell me

stories of my mother so that I can recapture a fuller picture her. I don't want those last years to be the final statement on her life.

The loss of a loved one to dementia or Alzheimer's is a silent, creeping grief. The person is present, but they aren't. One moment they may recognise us, the next we are a foreigner to them.

The loss of the person we once knew is also a situation faced by those dealing with a traumatic brain injury, mental illness, addiction, and other conditions. The person may become almost unrecognisable, but we still interact with them every day. They remain a part of our lives, but not as we previously knew them. The pain of this paradox is made worse when those around us don't realise that we are grieving.

When, for whatever reason, we lose the person we knew it doesn't necessarily change our level of attachment to them. We still love them but the nature of our relationship to them changes. Because there has often been a dramatic alteration in personality, this person no longer behaves as they did before. If, for example, the person is suffering from a drug addiction, their behaviour may become erratic and they might start stealing from others or us. We may also grieve for the life that the person is not living as all their energy focuses on living for their addiction.

The grief is not restricted to caregivers. The sufferer themselves may well grieve.

> Depression can feel like grieving for oneself. When my mental health gets bad, I miss and mourn the loss of the happy person I was – the loss of self. Even now, when my health is being managed well, I miss the person I was when I didn't feel like I had to manage my health and didn't have to look over my shoulder for that dark cloud.
>
> I also grieve for my lost time, especially when I see my peers, and those younger than me, passing me by when it comes to entering new phases of life. I spent many years stuck in places: stuck in bed; stuck in waiting rooms and waiting lists to get the help I needed; stuck begging for second, third, fourth chances; stuck in the quicksand of my mind. Severe

> mental illness robbed me of not only myself, but of the entirety of my youth. Sometimes the grief feels like it's going to swallow me.

Then grief may re-emerge in another form when mental health is recovered, and the person has to get to know themselves again. King Lear asked, 'Who is it that can tell me who I am?' For those experiencing the loss of their self, their grief is loaded with paradox. Philip has been diagnosed with early Alzheimer's.

> My journey through Alzheimer's continues to be marked with alternating times of bravery and fear, expectation and resignation, clarity alternating with frustrating confusion and one hell of a lot of paradox.

Positive changes can also generate grief when a person becomes different from the person we formerly knew.

> Allan experienced a life-transforming spiritual conversion, resulting in radical life-style changes. Some months later his parents called me. They explained that they were delighted in the new and far healthier life their son was leading. But they now struggled to relate to him. He no longer came around to have a beer with his family or attend the rugby with Dad. Something of the relationship they had with him had gone.

As we grieve a person still living it can be helpful to remind ourselves of why and how we love them, and to cherish the person they are while grieving the loss of who they were. The loss imposes an unwelcome change in our relationship, but we may be able to experience a creative relationship with them in new ways.

Living Loss and Disability

Disability occurs when someone with a long-term physical, mental, intellectual or sensory impairment experiences barriers that hinder their full participation and enjoyment of life. Disability results from the interactions between people with impairments and the attitudes and environment in which they live.[11]

Rebecca came into the family as a young foster daughter, having experienced profound and multiple forms of neglect and abuse. She now lives with cognitive functioning problems, memory issues, and chaotic attachment disorder. She has very poor understanding of cause and effect. To cope with this basket of psychological challenges, she has learned to hide her real self behind a convincing facade. As a result, all but her immediate family and close friends see only a 'normal' teenage girl.

> As she becomes increasingly aware of the challenges she faces, Rebecca grieves for the girl she could have been. She also grieves for the future her peers will have, but that she will struggle to attain. Few recognise this. Teachers and other adults have told her that she can't use the past as a reason for her current struggles. 'Be grateful for your foster family and stop living in the past.' They don't see what Rebecca struggles with and what she has lost.
>
> Her foster family also grieves. Not for one moment do they regret taking Rebecca into their family, but they pay the price of a living, ongoing grief. They must deal with all the difficulties and demands that come with nurturing a deeply damaged child.
>
> It's hard for her foster parents to watch their other children catch up and pass milestones Rebecca is still struggling with. 'It's a constant grinding ache that things had to be this way – that someone else messed up their kid so much that we had to step in. Sometimes I'm angry. Sometimes I'm overwhelmed with sadness. I fluctuate between the two. It's an emotional rollercoaster. If I hint to those outside the situation about how I feel, they invariably say: "But you have saved her,

---

11 This is a paraphrased definition taken from the Preamble to the United Nations *Convention on the Rights of Persons with Disabilities,* which recognises that disability is an evolving concept. https://www.un.org/development/desa/disabilities/convention-on-the-rights-of-persons-with-disabilities/convention-on-the-rights-of-persons-with-disabilities-2.html

imagine what it could have been like if you hadn't taken her in." Then comes the comment that minimises Rebecca's and our struggles: "All kids are like this." I'm always imagining what it would have been like if we hadn't taken her in, but I look equally at what we saved her from, and what we lost.'

Experiencing disability can involve a deep grief that may last for many decades. Disability can become a constant companion, an ongoing living loss, a recurrent grief.[12] A disabled person, as well as those who live with and care for people with a disability, may experience this. Yet it's common for this expression of grief to be frowned upon. Kenneth Doka encapsulates the issue: 'We admire people who take disability in their stride. We expect parents to love a child whatever the disability. To express grief often runs counter to these social values.'[13]

A parent loves the child deeply yet grieves the opportunities and experiences that the child will probably never know. 'It is the emotion-filled chasm between "what is" versus the parents' view of "what should have been."'[14] This is a grief rooted in the loss and discrepancy between the reality of how things are and the life we would dream of. Anna, who works with families and children living with disability, describes this divergence.

> One parent I have a close relationship with is suffering as her best friend's son moves into intermediate schooling – a milestone her son never met as he died a year ago. But she also grieves the milestones he never would have met anyway, due to his profound disabilities.
>
> The parents sometimes talk about the ongoing sorrow they feel, while at the same time learning to appreciate the child they have, who is not necessarily what they expected.

---

12 Sometimes referred to as chronic sorrow. See Susan Roos, *Chronic Sorrow: A Living Loss* (New York: Brunner-Routledge, 2002).
13 Doka, *Grief is a Journey*, 200.
14 'Living with Chronic Sorrow.' Accessed from: http://www.chronicsorrow.org/?page_id=11

Emotions frequently expressed by parents and caregivers include anger, frustration and confusion, and there is certainly no sequential order to this grief. It's always there in the background, yet interwoven with times of happiness and satisfaction, even joy. It's a loss commonly unacknowledged and misunderstood and those who don't understand deal out unhelpful and hurtful platitudes like 'How patient you are.' 'You've been specially chosen.'

When children and adults with a disability die, it's often assumed that the parents and caregivers of the person who has died will be relieved. Again, people trot out the platitudes. 'It's a blessing in disguise.' 'You can start living again.' The grief the bereaved experience, and the deep loving relationship they have forged, is disenfranchised. The loss is discounted.

Those with a disability may also experience grief. A person with a disability may be very aware of their parents' grief.

> I knew my parents grieved for the normal child they wanted. So, I grew up with guilt and shame for having denied them this. Later I knew resentment and anger. Instead of grieving for who I wasn't – who I couldn't be – could they not celebrate who I was and the abilities I had discovered?

To live with a disability, or with someone who has a disability, may sometimes mean that grief is a constant and complex companion. A parent with a child with intellectual impairment loves the child deeply, yet they also grieve the opportunities and experiences that their child will probably miss because of that impairment. It's common for their grief to surge at certain times. For example, when they receive an invitation to a friend's child's wedding or graduation. The invitation reminds them that their child may never marry or graduate. Yet the parents may feel bad that they are grieving and feel they should love and accept their child as they are. A person with a disability may also experience grief for what has been lost or may never be.

Relational Loss – Divorce and Dissolution

We are relational beings. Relationships sustain and shape us and constitute our deepest attachments. As we mature, we discover our identity in the setting of relationships. When, for whatever reason, a relationship ends, we know grief. It's a death, but unlike a physical death the other person is still alive. They are absent and present at the same time. This is particularly true when we co-parent. As Rabbi Rachel Barenblat explains, the relationship is 'ruptured but not gone... Once you've been attached to someone in a deep and intimate way, that attachment can't be erased. It becomes part of who you are. Even when the marriage is over, it remains, like a phantom limb... It is always something that used to exist, and its imprint remains.'[15]

The grief generated by a divorce (or as it's known under New Zealand law, a dissolution) is complex. It's the death of a relationship that may be decades old, and as with a physical death, the world as we know it shatters. The presenting loss is the ending of the marriage or civil union, but then there are multiple secondary losses, which frequently go unrecognised.

- Social and family loss – invitations dwindle as some of your friends or family members align themselves with your former spouse or partner and cease contact with you. Relationships change. You may feel humiliated by the circumstances and stigmatised.
- Parental loss – time spent with your children may change.
- Financial loss – property and financial resources are divided, and you will both probably experience a change (sometimes a drastic one) in your standard of living and financial security.
- Intimacy loss – sexual and emotional needs don't end because the relationship has, and yet you may find the idea of an intimate relationship foreign or frightening.

---

15 Rabbi Rachel Barenblat, 'Velveteen Rabbi'. Accessed from https://velveteenrabbi.blogs.com/blog/2017/03/on-divorce-and-ambiguous-loss.html

- Physical loss – routines end, and well-established patterns, ranging from walking the dog to cooking meals, paying the bills to mowing the lawns change.
- Future loss – shared dreams, plans, and commitments for the future come to an end.

The loss of the relationship may bring a high level of uncertainty into our life. What will life be like? Will I cope alone? For some, these unknowns can often seem worse than remaining in an unhappy, unhealthy relationship.

The grief generated by the ending of a relationship can be very complicated. While some people may experience relief and wellbeing, other emotions like guilt, resentment, and anger frequently run high and may be expressed by one or both parties in a very public way. Sometimes the partner who made the decision to leave the relationship is deemed by others to be at fault and is ostracised. Family members, friends, and members of the faith community may share in a blame game, not recognising that both parties are living with grief.

In addition, you may need to create a new relationship with your former spouse or partner. This is particularly important when children are involved and when custodial and access issues have to be resolved. It's not just hard on the couple getting divorced; the children are also deeply affected. They need constant reassurance that they are loved and are not the cause of the breakup of the relationship. Children also grieve!

In stories shared with me about grief experienced following a marital separation, a recurring source of hurt is the platitudes people utter and the unsolicited advice that's issued.

> Many people were only too willing to give me unwanted advice. 'You don't need a man in your life. You have your kids.' 'Don't go bringing a man into the house, that's not fair on the kids.' 'You should just go and get a full-time job.' (Easier said than done when you're a stay-at-home mum, and all of a sudden, your skills mean nothing in the workforce.)

Experiences of Disenfranchised Loss and Grief

In some faith communities divorced or separated persons are stigmatised, either overtly or covertly. When Raewyn and her husband separated, Raewyn encountered blatant judgement from fellow Christians, and was isolated from those she looked to for support.

> I wasn't allowed to grieve, and not surprisingly, I became depressed. In many ways I think it would have been easier if he had died, but instead he chose someone other than me. So not only was I grieving the loss of my marriage and partner, but also my self-esteem was attacked. All the while I was trying to say to the world, 'I'm fine.'

Religious belief left Helen feeling ambivalent about divorce.

> I was a good Christian girl who waited for marriage, and then dedicated myself to my husband and our relationship as I had been taught. He used that against me, and then abused me. I started experiencing severe grief long before we actually split, and I suffered in silence because I couldn't tell anyone. When we did separate, and I was honest with people about what had been happening, they just commented, 'Well, why didn't you get out sooner?' 'Why did you have a baby?' 'Why didn't you leave when he mistreated you while you were pregnant – surely you would put your baby first?'

> I believe marriage is lifelong, but once a child was here, I couldn't let him be exposed to that, so I left. But the grief caused physical symptoms, headaches, anxiety, constant crying, and fear. And I had to put on a brave face and pretend nothing was wrong, otherwise people didn't know how to handle me. At work, in the same year my marriage fell apart, a colleague's dog died, someone had surgery, someone else's mother died, another discovered they had cancer, a teenage daughter was diagnosed with depression, and another retired. They all received support in the way of hugs, care packages, dinners cooked, phone calls, emails checking up on them, people popping in on them. I got nothing. Even my closest friends avoided the topic. They knew what had happened and they didn't know what to do.

As Raewyn and Helen experienced, grief generated by the ending of a marriage or partnership can go unrecognised, and the grieving person receives no support. Even close friends may reject the loss, thus compounding it: loss is laid upon loss. In Christian circles people, not infrequently, pass judgment on the parties in a divorce, especially on the one who initiated the separation. For them grief is denied. As Peter, who instigated the separation put it, 'Those who are seen as bad people don't get to grieve.'

> I made the decision to leave my marriage and was regarded by some as morally deficient. In the months following only a couple of colleagues (who had themselves been through marital break-ups) expressed understanding of the grief I was experiencing. Assumptions were made about how I felt and about why I left the marriage. So, I shelved my grief. I had no right to grieve. It took me a decade before I finally allowed myself to grieve, and when I did, it was heart wrenching. My tears were for the death of my marriage, but also for the pain and loneliness I had known over the years as I had struggled to stay in the relationship.

Those going through a divorce experience grief, regardless of the reasons for the relationship ending, and regardless of perceived guilt.

Relational Loss – Ending of a Romantic Relationship

You don't have to have been married or been in a civil union to lose a significant relationship. Kenneth Doka cites a study of young adults that showed that 'just over a quarter of the large sample indicated that a romantic breakup was their most serious loss to date and eclipsed others.' Young adults are particularly vulnerable as they lack support systems. He goes on:

> Your grief may be minimised as you are urged to get over it and find someone new. Adolescents and young adults may even be told that they will experience such losses often as they grow – a statement as comforting as reminding a child who lost his first beloved grandparent that he will eventually grieve the surviving three![16]

---

16 Doka, *Grief is a Journey*, 203.

The grief experienced has some quite different dimensions from that generated by a divorce, especially if there are no children to the relationship and no need to divide property and financial resources.

Another potential difference involves social networks. As with a divorce, there will be changes in previously shared friendships. However, married couples (especially those whose relationship lasted many years) usually establish stronger links with their extended family, and these links are often radically altered after divorce. Having said that, I must emphasise that the grief at the ending of a romantic relationship is very real, though it is commonly disenfranchised, as shown in a parent's response to their 15-year-old son's situation.

> Ever since his friend dumped him Richard has been moping around the house. You'd think someone had died. I tell him to forget his friend. Anyhow, the friend wasn't right for him and there are plenty of other fish in the sea. He just needs to snap out of it and get on with life. Richard has to toughen up and stop feeling sorry for himself. It's just a part of growing up.

Not only is the grief disenfranchised, but so also the griever. Richard's lost relationship is not acknowledged, and the parent's response may well cause him to withdraw and inhibit him sharing his feelings.

Unrecognised Relationships

A significant form of disenfranchised grief occurs when our relationship with the person who has died, or been lost in some way, is not recognised or supported by others.

> Edward and David were partners for over twenty years, though they never entered a civil union. When Edward died, David received supportive care from his faith community, but Edward's family minimised the relationship between Edward and David and sought to cut David out of the proceedings relating to the disposal of the estate – suggesting that their relationship wasn't 'really that serious.'

> Bill and Madeline had been divorced for nearly 25 years and both had remarried. When Bill died, it was assumed by

members of the wider family that because the relationship had been severed long ago, Madeline would not be emotionally affected. Was it appropriate for her, Madeline wondered, to attend the funeral? In the end she didn't attend the funeral but was able to acknowledge the death at a mid-week service held in her faith community where she was able to talk about Bill and to share prayers together.

A marriage or civil union may end in dissolution, but at some point, one ex-spouse or partner will have to face the death of the other. It may be assumed that a former spouse or partner, particularly if the dissolution was some years ago, will have no significant grief. While the marriage or civil union is ended, the relationship isn't. Significant bonds may link them. They may have children and grandchildren in common. They may share friends and wider family relationships. Most significantly, they share a personal history and experiences, which probably entails painful memories and feelings, but it's also quite likely they have memories they cherish. What place does the former spouse or partner and members of their family, such as former in-laws, have at time of death? If they attend the funeral, where do they sit? What involvement do they have in the funeral rites? How are they expected to respond? Will the tributes to the dead person refer to them, and if so, how? It is, as Madeline found, an ambiguous situation.

We frequently retain friendships, perhaps from childhood, but our own grief is subordinated to that of the family of the deceased. We may work with a person for several decades, working in the same space five days a week and sharing lunch times and coffee breaks, but after their death, we receive little if any acknowledgment of the relationship. Friend-grief is as real as that experienced by family members, but frequently goes unrecognised. Yet the old saying, 'You choose your friends, relatives are thrust upon you' holds true. The loss of a friend can have an acute impact on us. Even a casual friendship, one that's based on walks to the supermarket or workouts at the gym can be experienced as an intense loss, especially if the connection was an integral part of our daily or weekly routine.

The Loss of a Companion Animal

The bond between a human and an animal is strong and resilient. The affection of an animal is unconditional, tolerating our imperfections. Who else accepts us 100% for who we are and loves us no matter what? Pets are much-loved companions who gift us with their trust and playfulness, simplicity and self-acceptance. For many, a pet is as much a member of their family as a human, and yet when they die people will say, 'When are you going to get another one?' 'It was just an animal.' But it wasn't 'just' an animal.

The relationship between a human and an animal is unique, and the grief associated with its loss of it is equally unique. Human-animal companionship is one of many relationships we are capable of enjoying, standing on its own. Barbara Meyers, a grief therapist, puts it succinctly: 'It is not more or less important than other relationships; it is simply different – worthy of affirmation, validation, and respect.'[17]

Within the space of a couple of weeks, Jessica's grandmother died, and Amber, the family pet dog, was euthanised.

> Some weeks I miss Amber even more than Grandma, not because I loved Grandma any less, nor because she was in any way a less significant part of my life, but because Amber was part of the framework of my day-to-day life. I still get really worried when the gate is open, and I put my slippers outside of Amber's reach when I take them off, because those are just minor ways that her constant presence shaped my life.

Amber's presence was integral to Jessica's everyday life. For a person on their own, the relationship with their dog may be multi-dimensional: a companion, a protector, a fitness coach, and a source of connection with others they meet on their walks. For some, a pet can be a reason to get up in the morning.

Ros has been around horses most of her life. She reflects on the uniqueness of the grief that we can experience when they die.

---

17 Barbara Meyers, 'Disenfranchised Grief and the Loss of an Animal Companion' in *Disenfranchised Grief: New Directions, Challenges, and Strategies for Practice*, Kenneth J. Doka (ed.) (Champaign, Illinois: Research Press, 2002), 251.

> Horses are large and fill a sizable space in our lives, so their absence leaves a physical as well as an emotional gap. Very often a horse has carried its rider safely and willingly on its back – a place where once predators dragged them to the ground to kill and eat. Why horses allow humans to invade this sensitive area is a mystery, but it brings us to a sense of gratitude for their big hearts and a strong emotional attachment.
>
> To sit astride a horse, galloping along beaches and across country requires trust from both parties; to reach out to a therapy horse while in a state of deep distress or depression also takes an act of faith that the horse won't trample on fragile emotions. To have loved a horse in these ways and then suffer the grief of its loss cuts deep, and yet too often that grief is belittled or minimised because it was 'just a horse.'

When one of Ros' horses dies, she uses ritual to help ease the pain of loss.

> I arrange the horse in a galloping position with mane and tail flying once it is laid in its grave, and then place a posy of flowers reflecting its character – bright colours for bold horses, muted colours for those gentle souls. It helps.

As ritual is important when one of Ros' horses dies, so it is when a pet rabbit dies.

> When my daughter was about nine, her rabbit Bodkin died. She didn't react very much, and I worried that she was suppressing her emotions, but then I observed something reassuring. On her arrival home from school every day for several weeks she visited Bodkin's grave, placing on it a 'bunny salad' of dandelion flowers and leaves, or lettuce leaves from the vegetable garden. She didn't talk about her ritual though I saw how it healed her heart.

For a child, the loss of a pet is often their first experience of death, and how adults in their life manage and respond to the loss can influence the child's grief responses in the years to come. Mindful of the child's developmental stage and being careful to invite and encourage, not to compel, the following approaches may be helpful (and are also, of course, applicable to adults).

- Don't dispose of the animal's body as though it had disappeared. Create rituals – anything from a formal burial in the garden to lighting a candle. You may offer a prayer and read a poem (perhaps one composed by a family member).
- Discuss with the children what they need to do and how they wish to honour the life and death of their pet.
- Teach and encourage grieving. If the adults are comfortable with expressions of grief, then children grow up knowing this is normal and acceptable.
- Don't replace the animal too quickly. Barbara Meyers has observed that a new animal may complicate grief because it places the family as well as the new puppy or kitten in a potentially compromising set of circumstances – 'the family may resent the new animal, and the animal may sense the resentment. A quick replacement may also teach children that animal life (and perhaps all life) is cheap and replaceable.'[18]

A complicating factor in the grief may emerge when the decision has to be made to euthanise a pet. The grief may become more complex, compounded by feelings of guilt and regret.

In some faith communities an annual service for the blessing of animals is held (around the Feast of Saint Francis – 4th October). On these occasions it's important to include in the prayers a remembrance for companion animals that have died, acknowledging the grief of their human friends. In my faith community people have the opportunity at that service to light a candle in remembrance of pets that have died.

---

18 Meyers, 'Disenfranchised Grief and the Loss of an Animal Companion' in *Disenfranchised Grief*, 256.

Joy Cowley captures what a pet can mean:

> I give special thanks to my creator
> for the friendship of animals in my life.
>
> I can't count the times God has loved me
> through small furred and feathered things,
> how often I've been taught through them,
> lessons of trust and playfulness,
> simplicity and self-acceptance.[19]

Material Losses

We get attached to things. We may believe that we shouldn't, but grief knows nothing of 'should-nots.' Grief over the loss of a material object is usually about far more than the monetary value.

> Like so many others who lived through the Christchurch earthquakes and aftershocks, I lost numerous material items. Most of the breakages didn't worry me at all, but during one aftershock a small ornament was smashed. As I picked up the pieces, tears came to my eyes. 'Stop being silly,' I said to myself. 'Why get all emotional about this thing?' But it was far more than a 'thing.' It was one of the first gifts my wife gave me.

Our reactions to the loss of a material item will depend on the meaning it has for us and sometimes it has various meanings and triggers multiple responses. A few days after his car was stolen from their garage Ross reflected on the experience.

> It was a beautiful Honda CRV Sport, the most comfortable vehicle we've ever owned. Right now, it's probably in some chop shop being broken down into saleable parts or perhaps it has been driven into a lonely place and set on fire. Isn't it funny how, even though it was just a collection of engineering and metal, I have a deep sense of loss and a concern for its whereabouts and wellbeing? Memories of journeys past are strangely tied to that vehicle.

---

19 Joy Cowley, 'Do Dogs go to Heaven?' in *Aotearoa Psalms: Prayers of a New People* (Wellington: Catholic Supplies (N.Z.) Ltd., 1990), #9.

> We bought this car from the profit we made through damned hard work. Sweat was turned into comfort, and it pulled our caravan. It took us on a number of memorable holidays, and it was a workhorse for countless trips to the dump or down to the shops. The empty garage feels a bit like a tomb. Now we have a sense of violation. Our home was entered, and our property was disrespected.
>
> I have a sense of anger and grief. In psychology, the two emotions are connected. From a Christian perspective I'm torn between two conflicting options. I could endeavour to walk in the moccasins of the perpetrator and have some empathy for his or her plight. Clearly, in some twisted way they feel justified in their actions and can rationalise the redistribution of our property. Yet, on the other hand, I want to throttle the little sod.

Ross refers to his sense of loss and grief as 'funny,' perhaps suggesting that it's out of order. Yet, that's how our society so often responds. 'Don't be silly. It's only a car.' 'You should be over it by now.' Yet Ross had the insight to recognise the grief he was experiencing.

A burglary, fire, or natural disaster – any event that in some way destroys our home – not only robs us of possessions but also of a sense of security and stability. It's a violation. In these experiences the fear and anger, which Ross identified, often cause us to overlook the grief experience. For some there is the belief that material possessions should not matter that much. In TV reports following the destruction of a home, a survivor often says: 'What matters is that we're alive.' That matters immensely, but in the weeks following, grief that accompanies the loss of possessions sinks in.

Nancy, who is a teacher, tells a story of a fire causing multiple disenfranchised losses.

> 'Our school suffered an arson attack. As a result, I lost most of my teaching resources as well as personal items. Both my parents had also been teachers, so I lost resources they had passed on to me. While valuable for teaching, those resources also had sentimental value. My class of 5 and

6-year-olds lost their work; some of them everything they had ever completed at school.

Friends, colleagues, family, and members of my church were generous with their time, money, and resources. The hard part was how senior management handled the situation. They were largely unsympathetic to the losses experienced by the children, the parents, and me. We were expected to deploy a "stiff upper lip." I was told the children and I could only discuss the fire on the first day back at school, after then it was "back to normal." I ignored that directive! We were denied access to Trauma and Crisis Teams when they came into the school

I was told to remove comments on several children's school reports referring to the fire; expressing my concern about how the child had reacted to the loss of personal possessions. I gambled on the fact that my reports would not be re-read so I didn't change the comments. The gamble paid off!

Staff members were denied information about the offenders and the process that was to be followed with them.

I was told I was wasn't a victim and was expected to carry on as if nothing had happened while trying to reorganise my resources, teach children who were confused, angry, hurt, and upset, to say nothing of dealing with my own feelings.

I needed to not only grieve for all the losses associated with the fire – the physical destruction of the buildings and contents – but also the often unthought-of losses, e.g. the Mum who was upset because her child's raincoat was destroyed and she had to find the money to purchase a new one; the folders containing a year's work for each child; the special picture a child had drawn; the questions from the children, especially why? and not being able to give them an answer.

My grief was compounded by the knowledge that the school I had worked in for many years was being unprofessionally managed and was later deemed "a school at risk."

Nancy was spiralling downwards, and no one seemed to notice except her husband and son. They both urged her to resign but Nancy held on, not wanting to leave her class and hoping that, somehow, she might 'fix things.' A colleague finally intervened by initiating contact with Victim Support. Consequently, Nancy wrote a victim impact statement, obtained information about the fire and the perpetrators, and resigned from her position. Nancy moved to another teaching position in another school, which became her 'healing place because it was a well-run, full of happy children, and a wonderfully co-operative staff who had great collegiality.'

For Nancy, and others affected by the fire, the presenting losses were the material objects destroyed in the fire. This initial loss, however, unleashed a series of subsequent losses: the experience of violation and vulnerability, the loss of relationships, loss of health, loss of a familiar work environment, and the loss of objects that represented significant memories and achievements.

Infertility and Childlessness

Couples who have difficulty conceiving go through pain that is all the more excruciating because it's silent pain.

> We had been trying to start a family for about three years. When we sought medical advice, I was tested. Finding out that I was infertile was profoundly painful. Later on, my psychologist talked with me about how that was a grief that had not been dealt with at the time. The loss was for the children that my wife and I were never to produce. It was a crushing blow to my sense of identity and my whole understanding of my purpose in life.

Another man writes:

> The grief associated with my infertility is hard to grasp. It's a strange loss because it's the loss of something that never was and cannot be – the loss of hopes and dreams – the loss of identity. I have several children though no birth children. Yet,

even decades later, this grief still strikes. I wonder – would a birth child have my eyes? I can still feel the inexpressible pain I knew when another child was baptised at church – when new parents or grandparents eagerly showed me their latest baby photos – when well-meaning friends would ask what our plans for a family were – when another month passed and it was clear my wife wasn't pregnant. Month after month of waiting – of hoping – of 'trying'. It's an intensely private grief.

Infertility is a deeply complex loss, as Louise explains.

Infertility is not so much a diagnosis as a retrospective description of circumstance. It is often not attributed to any cause, and its symptoms are the lack of something, a failure of the past to have provided something for the future.

As a grief, infertility has no event and no end. What is it that we are grieving for? What is the loss? It's not focused on a specific event or 'thing' but on the lack of something.

When there is no single cathartic moment which allows one to whole-heartedly give in to that grief, no way to point directly to something and say 'that, that is what I've lost,' then there is no means to assimilate grief. And when there is no publicly known event to create the expectation in others that we might be grieving, it becomes a private pain, and therefore somehow questionable, invalid: the grief can seem to be over nothing more than a cycle of trying and hoping and trying and hoping – and to grieve that seems faintly ridiculous.[20]

No words encapsulate the way infertility affects almost every aspect of our lives and relationships: home, sex, friends, family, hopes, and plans. You can't just say one word, as a person bereaved can, and expect some level of understanding.

---

20 Louise Williams, 'I know the pain of infertility - and talking about it helps'. Accessed from https://www.theguardian.com/commentisfree/2014/jun/06/i-know-the-pain-of-infertility-and-talking-about-it-helps

Experiences of Disenfranchised Loss and Grief

Childlessness can be because of infertility or miscarriage, because it's a choice made, because a child or children have died, because of estrangement, or because the right partner was not there at the right time.

> It was during the Good Friday service. I was sitting there, when suddenly tears flowed uncontrollably down my cheeks. They continued to flow without stopping for the rest of the service and for the hour following as I sat alone in the church.
>
> I was in my late thirties, single, never married and childless and all I longed for was to have children. For the next three days I wept and began my grieving for the children that might never eventuate. Over those days and the following months, I worked through and came to terms with the notion that if I did not get pregnant before I was forty-five years of age I could be sixty with a fifteen-year-old child or younger, and that would not be fair to either of us. So, the age of forty-five became my cut off-point.
>
> Whilst there was no bereavement, for no one had died, there was an acute sense of loss. A loss of what might have been, a loss of my sense of identity as a woman, and my hopes and dreams of being a mother. The loss of being seen by others as a complete person, and this especially includes how my brother and sister still exclude my thoughts and opinions when it comes to discussions about family. The reminders from people in the community who assume that I have children, and at my current age, that I have grandchildren and who suddenly don't quite know what to say. Not bereavement, but the grief and loss were real, and I needed to work through it.

Some women who are childless speak of a sense of shame that they had 'failed' as women. This reflects the need of others to define women by their children or lack of them, in a way they don't for men. For Mary, her grief involves the loss of 'life potential,' but also a loss of her place in society. As a woman without children she felt judged. She explains.

The world is set up to cater to couples and families. Every day you're reminded somehow of your 'lacking.' Society tells you – and I've had people say this to me – that you are less of a woman or not fulfilling your destiny as a woman by not having a child in your womb. It causes grief too as to how your loss affects others. I still feel guilt at not providing my parents with grandchildren and thank God my brother has had a daughter for them to dote over. And there's another reminder – when my parents gush over their granddaughter I feel the pain that they'll never be able to do that for a child of mine.

The griefs carry on and change as you age. After I had a hysterectomy at the age of 22, I received counselling, and came to terms with not being able to have a biological child. But when I was around 30 all my friends started having babies and a new kind of grief came over me. Not just societally, but within my own intimate circles, I was never going to fit in. I sometimes get left on the outer because I don't have children to bring to play dates or take to Mainly Music.

Mary's grief has taken her on a journey. 'I learned to stop listening to what society told me I should be and what I should value.' But like so many griefs, 'it's a lifelong grief that waxes and wanes.'

Those of us who know the grief of infertility and childlessness often feel it keenly when Mother's Day and Father's Day are commemorated, or when (as in the Anglican tradition) Mothering Sunday is celebrated. We all need to be acutely sensitive and recognise that not all are parents, and for many of those, it's not by choice.

- Don't assume someone is childless by choice.
- Don't assume that they are okay with it, but also (as with any grief) don't pity them.
- If you have children or grandchildren, be mindful of not always talking about the children in your life.

Experiences of Disenfranchised Loss and Grief

- Remember that asking someone if they have children can be a painful question.
- Be mindful of how many events (especially in church life) are 'family' orientated (translated: children) and consider how to include childless people.

Grief in Foster Care

Grief is rife in foster care. The child loses not only parents but also the world they know. Everything changes: daily routines and rules, surrounding environment, school, family and friends. The former environment may have been unhealthy and unsafe, but what was known no longer is. The foster parents experience grief. As Kenneth Doka says, they are given two paradoxical messages: 'Love the child as if he or she were your own and remember this is temporary care so do not get too attached!'[21] At the same time the relinquishing parents experience loss. They have lost their child and feel stigmatised. They have also lost control to a government agency and legal system.

Losses in Adoption

No adoption takes place without loss and grief. Three groups experience grief in adoption: the adoptee, the birth parents, and the adopting parents.

> I always knew I was adopted. At a young age I remember turning to my mother and saying, 'You can't tell me what to do. You aren't my real mother.' I was always aware of there being another world out there – somehow running parallel to what I was living. What was this other life like? Who were these other people who are my birth family? Why didn't they want me? Was I not good enough? My life was full of 'ifs'. I lived with a feeling of rejection, which carried through to adult relationships. I would always end them as a form of self-protection: 'I will reject you before you can reject me.'

---

21 Doka, *Grief is a Journey*, 207.

Another adoptee speaks of living with a parallel dimension in her life.

> I think of the person I might have been if I had grown up in my birth mother's family – a slightly different person, not me exactly, but a parallel me. The person who would have had my birth name. (I think birth names is another kind of loss.) So perhaps I grieve a version of myself, rather than grieving a loss of other people.

Adoptions involve a number of imaginary people who are mourned by each of the participants. The adoptee grieves their parallel self; the adoptive parents grieve their imaginary birth child(ren); and the birth parents grieve their imaginary version of the child that would have grown up with them.

In recent years a growing body of literature has begun to emerge around the grief experienced by adoptees. What is clear is that, as with all losses, grief experiences cannot be stereotyped. Many adoptees, however, struggle with feeling unloved or unwanted, and it's not uncommon for them to face issues of identity and heritage. Tough questions arise: 'Was I abandoned? Who are my "real parents" – my birth parents or my adoptive parents? Where do I come from?' The needs of adoptees include the assurance that they are worthy people; the assurance that their dual heritage (birth and adoptive) is valid; and the recognition that adoption can be good and painful and may present life-long challenges for all involved.

The birth parent grieves giving up their child. In the past many birth mothers were coerced into relinquishing their child and were left with deep feelings of guilt, shame, self-blame, and anger. Until open adoptions became possible, they were left wondering how their child was faring. 'What has become of my child, and if I meet her, will she forgive me – will she understand my decision – will she even want to know me?'

When a child dies, a parent's grief is acknowledged. The pain is accepted and expected, and people react with care and love. When a birth mother chooses to place a child for adoption, the loss of that child can be just as devastating.

> For birth mothers who lived in the era of mandatory closed adoptions, as I did, the separation of mother and baby is just as complete as if the child had died. The difference occurs because much of the time, the birth mother's grief is... often ignored or even forgotten.
>
> Like a parent whose child has died, a birth parent's grief is recurring. When the child would have been old enough to walk, you grieve over the loss of that experience. You grieve over the loss of the milestones of kindergarten, getting their first bicycle, watching them play on teams, graduation, and a wedding. Each milestone is its own loss that has its own grief.[22]

Researchers have suggested that the birth parents' grief is particularly complicated and intense because the birth parent knows that their child is alive and that there's the possibility that this grief need not be. 'Regardless of whether the birth mother participated in an open, mediated, or closed adoption, data analysis revealed the adopted child continued to be psychologically present for her, not only on special occasions such as birthdays, but as she went about her everyday life.'[23]

Adoptive parents face their own griefs. These range from infertility (which doesn't necessarily vanish because they now have a child by adoption) to the loss of a birth child, and perhaps the loss of the experience of pregnancy.

As the adopted child grows up they need the opportunity, support, and space to work through their grief and to explore their adoption and what it means for them. This often leads to the adopted child making contact with their birth parents – an action that can cause the adoptive parents to feel deep anxiety, perhaps fearing that they may lose their child: 'Having met their birth parent(s) will my child still see me as their parent?' While these questions and emotions

---

22   Lisa Taylor, 'Understanding Birth Mother Grief', 28 December 2015. Accessed from https://adoption.com/understanding-birth-mother-grief
23   K. March, 'Birth mother grief and the challenge of adoption reunion contact' in *American Journal of Orthopsychiatry* 2014, 409-419.

The Losses of Miscarriage and Stillbirth

Even though around twenty per cent of pregnancies end in miscarriage, they are rarely talked about. Having recently miscarried, Jule reflected on why this might be.

> Why, for many of us, does a miscarriage still feel like a dirty secret we would rather hide in our emotional cupboard? What are we afraid of? Confronting others with a difficult subject, overwhelming them with our loss, sadness and vulnerability? Making them uncomfortable, struggling for words? Or are we afraid of the judgement others could direct at us? That maybe others discuss behind our backs that they're sure… we may have brought it on ourselves? Is it our helplessness at dealing with the issue? … We think, if we do everything right, eat healthily, quit smoking, drinking… all should go well. Even if something goes wrong, modern medicine should be able to help us, right? Wrong. For most miscarriages there will be no explanation. They happen – in the majority of the cases – because of a genetic blip. They are seen as random, isolated events that will have no bearing on a woman's future chances of having a baby.[24]

A loss in pregnancy isn't a one-off event but an ongoing journey, as described by Suzy Liddell:

> There is the obvious grief that follows the actual miscarriage, but then there is grief that comes when we 'should be getting the antimony scan done today,' or grief when we 'should be preparing the nursery and buying a car seat,' or grief when we 'should be celebrating the birth of our new baby,' or grief when we 'should be celebrating Mother's Day and Father's Day' or the grief when we 'should be planning our baby's first birthday party,' or the grief when we see a child who's the age our baby 'should be'…

---

[24] Jule Scherer, 'Miscarriage isn't a dirty secret', 9 July 2014. Accessed from http://www.stuff.co.nz/life-style/parenting/pregnancy/conception/miscarriage/10248178/Miscarriage-isn-t-a-dirty-secret?rm=m

Experiences of Disenfranchised Loss and Grief

> In addition to all this grief comes the loss of innocence, which zaps the joy and excitement from every subsequent pregnancy. The two pink lines on a home pregnancy test don't bring the same happiness they did before; instead they bring fear, flashbacks, anxiety, sadness, and confliction… Do you allow yourself to build up hope which could then make the drop to despair even harder? Or do you guard your heart and deny yourself the happy anticipation that is totally natural during this time?[25]

A stillbirth, like a miscarriage, is a very lonely event that most women and men navigate in near seclusion. Not only is it the loss of life, but also the loss of hope and joy, the loss of what might have been. It is as Christina expresses it, 'a strange kind of grief. It's not grief for someone you know, but grief for someone you will never get the chance to know.'

> It's a strange thing recovering from a stillbirth. Your body is confused and still yearns for something that is missing. I struggled with my husband's lack of emotion, how he could return to work after only a few days and act like nothing had happened. I learnt however that distraction was his way of dealing with his pain. I returned to work six weeks later and I found the hardest part was people saying nothing at all…
>
> The grief of stillbirth does not go away but you learn to live alongside it. It has a tendency to rear its head unexpectedly and I still find myself occasionally crying myself to sleep. My faith in God has been severely tested. I have a feeling the rollercoaster ride has not ended, but I believe our faith will carry us through, whatever the outcome.[26]

A loss in pregnancy can be a complex grief, which is compounded when the mother and partner are faced with insensitive responses. 'At

---

[25] Suzy Liddell, 'My arms are empty, but I am still a mother,' 8 May 2017. Accessed from https://www.stuff.co.nz/stuff-nation/92325011/my-arms-are-empty-but-i-am-still-a-mother

[26] Christina Borthwick, 'The grief of not knowing our baby,' 3 August 2014. Accessed from http://www.stuff.co.nz/life-style/parenting/pregnancy/conception/miscarriage/10324023/The-grief-of-not-knowing-our-baby

least you didn't lose a real child.' ... 'You can always have another one.' ... 'You'll soon get over it.' ... 'You've got other children.' ... 'Never mind – these things happen.' The death of a baby, of whatever age or stage of development, is the death of an irreplaceable individual and the loss of a future. Statements that speak of the loss as 'being for the best,' which people often make when the child lost had a disability, are similarly insensitive.

Loss from Medical Termination

Within the church many people hold very strong views about abortion. As William Worden, a leading figure in grief studies and counselling, observes:

> Abortion is one of those unspeakable losses that people would rather forget. The surface experience after an abortion is generally one of relief; however, a woman who does not mourn the loss may experience the grief in subsequent loss.[27]

Some women who choose to have an abortion experience grief. Others don't. Some seek support and care many years later. Various factors may complicate and intensify grief, including an ambivalence about abortion, feeling constrained by age, circumstances, or finances; or seeing the pregnancy as a failed solution to a problem. A woman from a faith community that opposes abortion may have an agonising faith struggle. The decision to terminate may also generate grief in fathers and prospective grandparents.

> Termination isn't something discussed in polite circles. Only one person has ever acknowledged my grief over the death of my daughter. It's like she never existed to anyone but my husband and me. She was never going to be born alive, and yes, while we made the choice, it hurt like hell and it still does. The grief afterwards drove me to the brink of suicide. What gets to me is that we have nowhere to go. There's no grave, and the thought of her tiny body being disposed of... like a piece of rubbish, is something I can't handle and so I block it out. But she isn't rubbish. She lived in me and a part

---

27 William J. Worden, *Grief Counselling and Grief Therapy: A Handbook for the Mental Health Practitioner*, 4th Ed. (New York: Springer Publishing, 2009), 200.

> of her still does in the form of grief and buried tears that I let no one see.
>
> My faith made it harder as good Christian women don't terminate their babies, and if they do, they have to keep quiet about it and never mention it, as it's not seen as acceptable.

As a pastor my paramount concern is always non-judgmental care for a person who is grieving, whatever the cause of the loss. Occasionally in my parish ministry, women who have experienced the loss of a child by medical termination or miscarriage, have asked for help as they wrestled with their grief. In response I have sometimes offered a very simple service that usually includes the ministry of healing, a naming of the child, and the commendation of the child into God's care. The women always reported a sense of peace and acceptance of their loss and some spoke of being able to give the dead child a new-found place in the life of their family.

> I was in my mid 20s. When I found out I was terrified. I knew I couldn't cope with being a mother at that stage. So I decided to have an abortion. At first, I felt relief. But then there was this sadness. It wasn't something I could talk about with my family. They had made very clear what they thought about women who had abortions. It was confusing – relief, sadness, and then quite a bit later, guilt kicked in. Through it all I felt so alone. Isolated. A few years later, when I was finally able to talk about it with my Vicar, I was able to identify other feelings, like regret and shame. There were so many emotions – all mixed up. When my Vicar talked about grief it made sense. Most importantly, I was finally able to talk about it and not be judged and condemned. It was like I had spent these years walking around with a sharp stone in my shoe. Now the stone was removed, and I could stand up tall.

Loss of Employment

When we meet someone the first questions often asked are, 'What family do you have – how old are your kids?' and 'What's your job – where do you work?' Unemployment and infertility may be two of the most commonly unacknowledged losses. Both challenge our sense of identity and worth.

> I was made redundant. They called it downsizing and organisational restructuring, but it meant the same thing – I was fired. The redundancy package was okay, so with cutbacks in the household budget we managed until I got another job. But it knocked me sideways. I'd given my best to the organisation – invested my time, energy, and life in it. My job gave purpose to my life. Redundancy meant that I wasn't valued. I was no longer wanted – not needed. And I missed my colleagues – people who really mattered to me.

Like other losses, the loss of employment generates various secondary losses. The loss of a job is not only the loss of income (the most obvious loss), but also the loss of identity, of self-worth, meaning, and purpose in life. Then there's the loss of companionship and social standing. Because we often define ourselves by our work, to lose employment leads to diminishment of self-esteem, and we might struggle to find meaning and purpose in life. It may be necessary to apply for an unemployment benefit, which many people experience as a demeaning process, compounding the loss of self-esteem.

For some, especially if a healthy redundancy package is given, redundancy may be welcome, offering the opportunity to explore new avenues. Likewise, retirement may be welcome. Many of us enter retirement with delight, even a sense of relief, but then we experience various losses: our income level diminishes, relationships are lost, and our daily routine changes. The world as we have known it for possibly five or more decades has gone, and as Felicity recounts, we find that we are not indispensable.

> One week, I'm racing round work, one meeting after another, 55 emails to answer before lunchtime – people bombarding me with endless questions. The next week – nothing. No meetings, no frantic emails, no demands at all. The long and scary silence of retirement has struck… Like many my age, I'm betwixt and between, not ready to be fully retired, and therefore not fully free to come and go as I please. That's because I still crave a sense of belonging, of being useful and

being needed, of fancying myself indispensable. Pulling me the other way is the desire for freedom, to just up sticks and see the rest of the country… What is it, this pull back to busy-ness? It's not the money. It's the fear of that long and scary silence when one day everyone wants whatever it is you can offer and the next day, you're forgotten.[28]

Work is the primary source of identity for many of us and absorbs our best energies and creativity, so retirement is a major transition; it's a significant change, and change spells loss. Who am I now? What is my place in society? What is my value? Where do I put my energy and creativity? Life has to be reconstructed, and we grieve as we work to find a new normal.

Loss through Abuse

Abuse, in whatever form it takes, results in multiple and profound losses. These losses include loss of innocence, loss of childhood or youth, loss of faith, loss of hope, loss of family relationships, loss of self-esteem and self-belief, loss of personal power, and loss of the ability to experience pleasure. Survivors frequently express a deep loss of 'who I could have been if I had never been abused.' 'If I hadn't been abused, how would I be different?' 'If I wasn't living with this life-sentence, who would I be?'

> The grief I know isn't so much linked to the actual event of abuse but to the loss of my childhood. I see children being carefree, holding nothing back, simply being themselves, and I grieve for the freedom I never experienced.
>
> I also grieve the fact that for years I looked the other way as my inner child reached out in pain and hurt. I grieve the things she missed out on because, as an adult, I was trying to protect myself from what I knew she wanted to tell me. I grieve that I abandoned her and denied her the right to the freedom she longed for.

---

28   Felicity Price, 'Semi-retirement: Can you really have the best of both worlds?' Accessed from https://www.stuff.co.nz/southland-times/life-style/93463830/Semi-retirement-Can-you-really-have-the-best-of-both-worlds

Another survivor writes:

> The abuse I experienced over 40 years ago never goes away. It will suddenly, without warning, raise its ugly head. It will always be a part of me. I can't erase it from my story. There are still occasions when I feel anger towards my abusers. What did I lose? I lost my innocence. I lost trust. I lost belief in myself. I lost self-esteem, self-worth, and sense of dignity. I know some healing for the wounds the abuse left, but the scars remain, and the grief lives on. As the years advanced, I've learned not to focus on the violations I experienced, for that would leave me trapped in a time warp that I can't change. I'm learning to grieve my losses, and as I do, I'm beginning to embark on a journey which is leading me to discover new meaning in my loss – to discover God who shares it with me. But… it still hurts. It always will.

Discovering Disenfranchisement

Carol's story is one of discovery, recognising and owning her losses and griefs.

> Disenfranchised grief – it's when your heart is grieving but you can't talk about or share your pain with others because it is considered unacceptable to others. It's when you're sad and miserable and the world doesn't think you should be, either because you're not 'entitled' or because it's deemed not 'worth it.'

> As much as my grief was ignored and deemed unacceptable to others, the damage occurred when I denied myself permission to pay attention to my own story of loss and gain. Over three decades ago I married my husband. He was born and raised in the home where we live in rural New Zealand. New Zealand is not my country of birth. I was born and raised in the Northern Hemisphere in an urban setting.

Carol identified several arenas in her life most affected by disenfranchised grief: country and culture, family, sense of belonging and roots, climate, career success, friendships, loss not validated by the people she loved the most, and her expectations of marriage and family life.

> I married into a family who hold the privileged responsibility of being part of the building blocks of rural life in New Zealand. My husband's ancestors established a grand legacy for their descendants. Because my new life and new marriage in New Zealand was admired and openly envied, I didn't feel eligible when it came to the negative emotions associated with loss. In my community it's not unusual to hear the comment 'Oh well... never mind.' This single comment has created many moments of confusion, which, in turn, has led to cognitive dissonance. My heart ached and grieved the loss in the arenas mentioned before. However, my head ran a recording reminding me how lucky I was. In essence, I denied my own heart in an attempt to hold it together so I could get along in my new life.
>
> I've wrestled with my own expectations. As with all loss, catharsis is inevitable. In my case it has taken a long time. Currently I feel stronger as I can now understand that there was no malicious intent in the comments and expectations I felt from others. Those people simply didn't understand my world.
>
> The trick now is to create my own boundaries about how I interpret situations and other people. I do have a wonderfully supportive husband, healthy children, fantastic friends, and I'm grateful for the support I've received from medical professionals. Asking for support has been critical.
>
> Going backwards to go forward can sometimes be viewed as self-indulgent, but in my case, the catharsis was essential to experience in order to move forward.

Change and Transition

In the journey of discovery described above, Carol identified how grief can entail both loss and gain. That's the nature of the flux of life. We arrive and depart, grow and decline, achieve and fail, and every change involves loss and gain. We relinquish the old and accept the new.

> I accepted a new position which meant that we moved cities. It's been a very good move and I don't, for one moment, regret the decision. Yet I grieved for many things – for the loss of my community at the gym where I worked out several times a week, friends who I could call on and have a coffee with. I even felt the loss of my hairdresser and the familiarity of our supermarket – the loss of people, places, and routines that had become integral to my life. Sure, they were small losses and the grief was relatively easy to cope with, but they were, nonetheless, losses. I had to farewell the familiar in order to greet the new.

Change and transition, however positive, has an undercurrent of loss. We grieve when the balance of our lives is upset and the coping mechanisms that we use to deal with the demands of daily life are thrown out of kilter. Grief may accompany any change, even those we welcome or have initiated. Something which may be imperceptibly valuable to us has been lost. Our identity and life story have been disrupted. The world as we know it has changed and for a time we are disoriented. This is the grief of new gains.

- Receiving promotion at work or accepting a new responsibility
- Embarking on a new venture
- Acquiring personal independence
- Beginning a new relationship
- Welcoming a new member into our family
- Growth in our faith community

Kenneth Doka illustrates the grief of new gains.

> At graduation, you celebrated your achievement and looked forward to the next phase of life. Yet you also recognised

> you're leaving behind friends and teachers, and places and activities. There are also implications arising from the birth of a child. You may have anticipated the event for years and be overjoyed in the birth of new life. But you also know life will be different now; over the next couple of decades, your freedom will be limited – and for a shorter period, so will your sleep.[29]

In gaining what is new, the familiar has been lost. Our world as we knew it has ended. A Tibetan master said, 'Death is alive in life as change.' We experience a death whenever we experience change, and change is a constant: things change, people change, minds change, hearts change, beliefs change; life is change.

Some changes affect us more deeply than others. Some we readily embrace, such as a new relationship, a new and exciting work, or a new insight that changes our beliefs and outlook on life, while others we resist. Some changes emerge from within us, like a whispering desire or growing discontent. Others thrust themselves on us, uninvited, as from nowhere, cutting across our lives, shattering what we hold dear.

Our attitude towards change is influenced by whether we are initiating it (in which case we normally support it) or someone else is imposing the change upon us (which tends to make us resistant, resentful, even rebellious). When we experience imposed change, and even when we know it's ultimately a good thing, we struggle with it because it shows that someone or something else has control and has the power to cut across our lives and destroy or disrupt the familiar that gives us a sense of security. But whether the change is of our making or not, whether we embrace it or resist it, change means the loss of what we know.

We underestimate the impact change can have on people's lives, including our own. When we are either the initiators or collaborators of change, we are convinced of its rightfulness. We can see the gains that will be achieved; we know the good it will bring, and we may become impatient with those who reject the change and struggle

---

29 Doka, *Grief is a Journey*, 209.

The Grief Walk

with adaptation. But change of any kind, even change that we readily embrace, involves loss; the loss of what we knew, of what made life safe and familiar, and loss results in grief. Life is full of farewells to what has been, like the stage of helping children and grandchildren grow up.

> I felt the loss when each of the grandchildren became adult. Suddenly I was aware that they were independent, past the stage of needing help with homework, an ear to unload the home problems onto, and advice on teenage matters or even insistence on various rules of life. They no longer turned up on my doorstep to enjoy Grandma's baking. They weren't around to help (and learn) in the garden or in the house. I couldn't call on them, or they on me, in the way we always had before. I had been so lucky to have the chance to be their helper and protector; the wiser older generation with advice on how to do or manage whatever was going on in their world. Work and partners had taken over most of my roles. The need for me had lessened.
>
> That loss, however, has been made up for with the entry into my life of the new adult friends and confidants. Looking back on earlier times is lovely, the present with the enjoyment of their more occasional company is lovely and looking forward to being in and seeing what life has ahead for the grandchildren is very special. Loss is the beginning of something new.

In addition to the examples of disenfranchised grief that I've described there are, of course, countless other experiences of loss that people either misunderstand or don't acknowledge. What I've shared in this chapter reminds us that grief is not so much about death as it is about loss. Anything that we have, we can lose; anything we love can be taken away from us; anything that we are attached to, we can be separated from.

4 – Understandings and Misunderstandings about Grief

Our Loss and Grief is Unique – so Forget the Rules

> I'm fed up with well-meaning friends who tell me what stage I'm at in my grief. They don't know what it's like to be me. They haven't a clue what I'm going through.

This frustration, expressed by a widow just a couple of months after her husband's death, encapsulates a common misunderstanding about grief. Our grief doesn't follow a predetermined path. Knowing this gives us the freedom to traverse the grief walk in a way that's authentic for us.

Loss is a universal experience, but our grief isn't. Our grief is like our fingerprint, unique to us alone. There's no right or wrong way to grieve. There are no rules that make one person's reactions and responses normal and another's abnormal. It would be so much easier if grief were predictable and we could say, 'This is the path you'll walk; this is how long it will take; this is what you're going to experience.' But no, grief is unpredictable, complex, and messy.

Everyone's experience of grief is different just as every loss is different. No two people will grieve in the same way. Our relationship, for instance, to someone who has died, is utterly unique, and so how we grieve is equally unique. A parent dies, but each child in the family has a unique relationship to that parent, and so each child experiences the loss in a different way.

Our way of grieving, or style of grief, is influenced by various factors, which may include:

- our past experiences of loss and grief
- our life story
- how others in our family have modelled grief to us

- our personality
- our cultural background
- our age
- where we are at in terms of self-awareness and personal development
- our beliefs
- the support and understanding we have from others
- the significance and context of the loss and the changes that it will bring to our life.

It's inappropriate for me or anyone else to say, 'This is how you should grieve.' There's no standard path, no rulebook, no set timetable that you must follow, and there's certainly no universal remedy to instantly take the pain away.

While there is no 'right' way to grieve there are common patterns and elements to grief. But how you experience them and choose to respond to them is unique to you. You may, for example, not cry at all, or you may cry a lot. Some people find that the intensity of grief lasts a long time while for others it lasts for less time. At the end of this chapter is a section entitled 'We Grieve in Our Own Way – So Forget the Stereotypes,' in which I offer an approach to appreciating the different ways in which we grieve.

The grief walk takes a route that's far from straight. C. S. Lewis described it as 'like a long valley, a winding valley where any bend may reveal a totally new landscape.' But not every bend reveals something new.

> Sometimes… you are presented with exactly the same sort of country you thought you had left behind miles ago. That is when you wonder whether the valley isn't a circular trench. But it isn't. There are partial recurrences, but the sequence doesn't repeat.[30]

---

30 Lewis, *A Grief Observed*, 47.

It's a walk of discovery as we work out what we need to do, learning what is helpful and what is unhelpful to us, what is healthy and what is harmful. For instance, following a significant loss you may well find that you are in survival mode and your primary need is to get from here to there, from today to tomorrow. A mother whose young son had died was often asked, 'How are you doing?' Her reply, 'I'm doing.' As she explained, 'That's all I can manage. I can do – that's all.' In your grief, you are the one that matters, and I encourage you to do what you need to do. Many of us, probably most, rely heavily on social conventions, and use these to determine how we ought to behave in the wake of a loss. I suggest a different yardstick, which may be more helpful at this juncture: is this thought, this action, this response, helpful or harmful to me as I survive this time of grief?

It's likely there will be times, probably many times, when we feel lost and disoriented, for grief is a turbulent experience, affecting all aspects of our lives. Knowing that there isn't a set path that we must follow allows us to experience our grief in a way that's real for us. Grasping this simple but critical fact enables us to help ourselves and to appropriately care for and support others who are grieving.

There's No 'One Size Fits All' – so Forget Stages in Grief

When I speak with people about the uniqueness of loss and grief, the response is nearly always, 'Of course it's unique! How can it be anything else?' Yet there lingers the idea that grief is a linear process in which we grieve in a sequential manner following a series of predetermined stages – an understanding that negates the complexity and uniqueness of our grief experience.

This notion of stages in grief is rooted in a simplistic interpretation of the pioneering work undertaken in the late 1960s and early 1970s by Elizabeth Kübler-Ross. Based on her research working with terminally ill patients Elizabeth devised a model that reflected common reactions to dying. The model contains five stages that people go through: denial – anger – bargaining – depression – acceptance.[31] Psychologists, counsellors, pastors, and the general

---

31 Elizabeth Kübler-Ross, *On Death and Dying* (New York: Macmillan, 1969).

public readily accepted this model as the 'normal' way to grieve over a death; then in time it was expanded and applied to any loss. It was assumed that if we grieve well, then we ought to pass through these five stages (and in that order). If a person doesn't, then they are not grieving 'correctly'. This stage model, or various forms of it, is still frequently upheld as the norm, even though it's now widely accepted among grief researchers, counsellors, therapists, and pastoral theologians that there is no universal prescription for grief.

A prescriptive template for how we ought to grieve adds to the burden that grieving people are already carrying. It can also invoke a sense of guilt, leading them to think that they aren't grieving 'well enough.' A young man whose father had died came to me and announced, 'I'm grieving all wrong. I read this booklet that told me I should be feeling angry by now. But I don't. What's wrong with me? Can you show me how to grieve properly?'

Stage models can also become a checklist which answers the need for ready solutions and easily followed steps to relief. 'I've done the denial and anger, now onto to the bargaining. Been there – done that. Now I can move on.' But grief can't be dispensed with so easily. We must learn to live with our losses and sometimes that's a journey that takes a lifetime. Even if we have known significant losses before, this one is different. It's distinctive.

We may well experience one or more of the reactions described by Elizabeth Kübler-Ross as 'stages' (and we may even experience them in that order), and we may not. We may also experience several at one time, and we may revisit them over time. But most disquieting about this and other stage models of grief is that they lead those around the grieving person to think they know what the person is going through and that they can tell the person what to expect next.[32]

---

32 For an evaluation of Kübler-Ross' work see Ruth Davis Konigsberg, *The Truth About Grief: The Myth of Its Five Stages and the New Science of Loss* (New York: Simon and Schuster, 2011). For a brief article, see Ruth Davis Konigsberg, 'New Ways to Think About Grief', 29 January 2011.
http://content.time.com/time/magazine/article/0,9171,2042372,00.html

Understandings and Misunderstandings about Grief

A stages theory says grief works like this:

Loss occurs – denial – anger – bargaining – depression – acceptance.

It's a straight line, ─────────────── which is very neat and tidy. But grief is messy, very messy, and it's more like this:

When a loss occurs, our grief walk isn't clearly laid out. I experience it as a stumbling walk that has right turns, left turns, U-turns, roadblocks and dead ends, until gradually we learn a new reality, a new way of being in life without the physical presence of the loved one, or without the place, the friends, the relationship that meant so much. Grief is unpredictable and breaks like a storm over us, and then calms, seemingly without reason.

We are attracted to models of grief that lay out a clear pattern for how we grieve because grief is such a chaotic experience. These models give us a sense of order and control in a time of disorder and disempowerment. Empowerment can be discovered in the midst of grief, but not by slavishly following models of grief that deny the uniqueness of our experience or that imply that one day our grief will be eradicated.

We owe a debt to Elizabeth Kübler-Ross, for in her time she brought death and grief out of the closet, and at one level the stages of grief make sense. It gives us a sense of security at a time when life is in a state of turmoil. However, more recent research shows that the model doesn't match what people actually experience.

Two people who know the depths of grief from the inside offer these comments. Lucy Hone, whose twelve-year old daughter was killed in a road accident in Canterbury, writes, 'Grieving is no linear progression (meaning you start at A and work your way to Z); it's more like an exhausting, frustrating and ghoulish game of Snakes and Ladders (back and forth, up and down).'[33] Bryan Guy, whose

---

33 Lucy Hone, *What Abi Taught Us* (Auckland: Allen & Unwin, 2016), 12.

The Grief Walk

son Scott was murdered near Feilding, learned that grief is devoid of rules. 'Although psychologists categorise grief as possessing various stages… Bryan found they actually lacked sequence. The family bounced between each predicted stage like a Karaoke ball.'[34]

There is no 'one size fits all' way to respond to loss. I'm not even prepared to talk about grief as a process. It's too glib as it suggests that grief is something we do or go through that has a clearly defined beginning, middle and an end. A different way of seeing grief is in terms of a spiral in which we may experience or view these feelings and reactions many times, each time from a different angle or level.

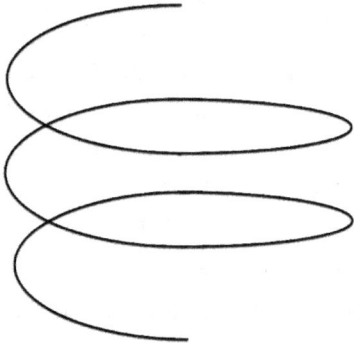

As time passes, we journey through our reactions to the loss many times, each time from a different perspective or place or time.

We Wax and Wane – so it's Okay to Retreat from Time to Time

In contrast to stage models, there's an understanding of grief in which we oscillate backwards and forwards, at times confronting and entering our pain, at other times moving away from it, even avoiding it. We may also experience, as Richard and Tracy did, contrasting emotions at the same time.

> It came as something as a shock to Tracy and me that we could laugh out loud *and* grieve our lost son at the same time. Other bereaved parents may come to the same realisation in the enjoyments of music, sex, or work… We began to

---

34 Tony Farrington, *Scott Guy: His Parents' Story of Love, Betrayal, Murder and Courage* (Kerikeri: Antares Publishing, 2013), 78.

realise... that other loves would form a supporting web of new tissue and cartilage around this irreplaceable loss.[35]

In the early period of our grief, the loss dominates, but as time goes on, we oscillate back and forth, at times facing our grief, at others withdrawing from it in order to gain some respite. Some days we are strong enough to deal with it, confronting the reality of our loss. At other times it can become all too much, so we immerse ourselves in work, in a hobby, in friendships. Two researchers, Margaret Stroebe and Henk Schut, describe this as 'dual process.' As they put it: 'The person may choose to take "time off," be distracted, or need to attend to new things, or at times it may be too painful to confront some aspect, leading to voluntary suppression.'[36]

Distraction, or taking time off, is an important element in grief, though one that isn't often talked about. This may be because in Elizabeth Kübler-Ross' model it would be considered as denial, but as T. S. Eliot wrote, 'humankind cannot bear very much reality.'[37] We need respite from the pain of grief. Distraction isn't a matter of hiding from the reality, but an aid to recovery. These small distracting activities also serve another purpose. We can use them as a bridge to help us return to the world, coming to terms with the reality of our loss and learning to live with a new normal.

Lucy Hone quotes Claire Rushton, whose 16-year-old daughter died of meningitis, and who found this dual process helpful.

> 'There are days that I just can't move and I don't want to, I just want to sit and be sad and for the world to stop.' But she's found her own way of drawing herself back... 'I tell myself... okay, you've cried now, now you need to get up and do something. I call it the "cleaning out the teaspoon drawer moment." I have come to realise that by giving myself permission to be sad and grieve, but also giving myself a reason to take me out of that grief, even if all I'm

---

35 Richard Lischer, *Stations of the Heart: Parting with a Son* (New York: Vintage Books, 2013), 234.
36 M Stroebe and H. Schut, 'The dual process model of coping with bereavement: Rationale and description', *Death Studies*, 1999, 23(3), 216.
37 T. S. Eliot, 'Burnt Norton' in *Four Quartets* (London: Faber and Faber, 1966), 14.

doing – cleaning the crumbs from the teaspoon drawer – I've moved, and that movement switches my emotions from despondency to a purpose again.'[38]

The teaspoon drawer is a helpful metaphor for the activities that can be used by the grieving person as a bridge to help them to re-enter the world.

A Continual Presence Which can Ambush us – so Forget the Timeline

Grief comes and goes on its own calendar and in its own ways. It's not an illness that runs its course. Rather, grief winds its way through our life and there's no way to predict its course or time or when and where it will affect us. It takes as long as it takes and lasts as long as it needs. There isn't a prescribed time for grieving; any more than there is for falling in love. When we lose who or what we love, there's no logic that can be applied or formula that can be used in determining how long it will last. And yet we do just that. It's not uncommon for those around a grieving person to say, 'He should be over it by now.' … 'It's about time she moved on.' … 'Obviously he's stuck in his grief.' Such comments assume there's a definitive end point when we are done with grieving. It's a very common misunderstanding that by one year we should be 'over it' and back to normal.

I'm often asked, 'Will my grief come to an end?' Some will say, 'yes;' others speak of learning to live with their loss; and yet others, many others, say that the grief is always a part of their life. I experience grief as being like a large iron nail, embedded into the trunk of a tree. The nail remains in the tree, for it can't be extracted, but over time the tree gradually grows around and over it, adding new layers of growth as each year passes, incorporating the nail into its life.

Our grief changes and the acuteness and pain soften over time as we learn to live with this new normal that's now part of who we are. This loss means we will never be the same again. This is why the idea of closure is a lie, even though people are so attracted to it. The loss, the absence, can be a continual presence, even decades later or

---

38 Hone, *What Abi Taught Us,* 101.

to the end of our lives. Another image for our grief is that it's like a new character in the story of our life. As our story develops the character grief recedes into the wings, and we may even forget that it's there. But it never fully vacates the stage and is capable of making an entrance at particular moments throughout the story of our life.

We will have good days and bad days, days when we feel the weight of our loss. Some tough days are almost predictable: perhaps an anniversary or days or seasons of significance. Another loss, either in our own lives or observed in someone else's life, may trigger our grief. On occasion we are being ambushed by our grief. It comes to us seemingly out of nowhere.

> I was happily pushing a trolley round the supermarket the other day and then a song came on that brought back a particular memory, and bang… the rest of the shopping was done with tears running down my face.

In one her novels Donna Léon describes this experience.

> It's always the odd, unpredictable things that set us off, Brunetti thought. Grief lies inside us like a land mine: heavy footsteps will pass by it safely, while others, even those as light as air, will cause it to explode.[39]

Grief can ambush us. There's no one strategy to prepare us for the grief ambush, but knowing that it's likely to happen, it may derail us less and help us to weather the ambush when it next occurs. The grief ambush can happen many years later, as this narrative illustrates.

> I was watching a movie and suddenly a short scene, lasting just a couple of minutes, triggered a grief. I felt as if I'd been blindsided – emotionally hijacked. At first, I felt foolish. It was a loss that was many decades old, and I thought I'd dealt with it. But here it was, demanding my attention. I spent some days pushing the experience away, but finally some inner wisdom led me to give this loss the care it sought. I entered the pain, and for the first time wept for the loss I had experienced.

---

39 Donna Léon, *Earthly Remains* (London: William Heinemann, Penguin Random UK, 2017), 200.

> Thinking about this loss now, I know its reality, but it's not raw. More like a long sadness that I know will always be a part of me – a grief that's been tempered as my life has grown around it. There are times when it comes to the fore, and the sadness is deep, but now I've given it a place in my life. I have allowed it to be.

Forget the timeline, although the intensity of our grief usually diminishes over time. There will be days when the agonising grief feelings return, but overall its average intensity reduces. The tough days will come less often, will become less intense, and will not last as long. Although grief can be without end, in time it looks different and hopefully more peaceful.

Hilary Smith, a poet and ordained minister, reflects on the grief ambush and our need to withdraw.

> **ambushed**
>
> Strange the way
> triggers return me
> to the shadows.
>
> When life seems calmer
> stable
> more days of coping better,
> a sharp word
> a glance
> a thoughtless remark
> a stressful demand of my energies
> and my defences crumble.
> Don't show it
> still fragile.
>
> I withdraw to a safe place
> and tend my wounds.[40]

---

40 Hilary Smith, *Grief's Shadowed Path: Poems of Loss and Healing* (Napier: EVBooks, 2017), 64.

Continuing Bonds – So Forget about Having to Let Go

Sigmund Freud contended that grieving involved gradually withdrawing all emotional energy from the dead loved one so that the bereaved person could invest in new relationships. Any sense of continued attachment to the dead person was deemed unhealthy. Healthy grieving, in other words, was all about letting go. When a person dies, they are dead and gone. They are no longer a part of our lives.

In recent years researchers have done an about turn on this idea as we realised that we have the emotional energy to create new relationships while maintaining an adjusted and redefined relationship with a loved one who has died. Rather than detachment from the dead we can maintain a continuing bond with them. Death does not bring an end to the relationship but changes it. This continuing bond with the dead can be understood and experienced in different ways. We retain memories that continue to inform, influence, and nurture us, and those who have died become a part of the ongoing story of our lives. After all, how can we separate ourselves from those who have died? They leave an indelible mark on who we are and how we see ourselves. Being my parents' son, being my uncle's nephew, being my grandparents' grandson, helps shape the person I am.

A grief researcher expresses the idea of continuing bonds thoughtfully.

> We can continue to 'have' what we have 'lost,' that is, a continuing, albeit transformed, love for the deceased. We have not truly lost our years of living with the deceased or our memories. Nor have we lost the influences, the inspirations, the values, and the meanings embodied in their lives. We can actively incorporate these into new patterns of living that include transformed but abiding relationships with those we have cared about and loved.[41]

Death may have physically taken our loved one, but they will always remain in our heart and mind and the gift of their life continues to give and to be appreciated by us. It's not uncommon for bereaved

---

41 Thomas Attig, *How We Grieve: Relearning the World*, revised ed. (New York, NY: Oxford University Press, 2011), 189.

people to experience extraordinary moments of connection with a dead loved one, such as a sense of their presence or in a vivid dream. Richard Lischer describes such an experience after his son's death.

> Within a few weeks of Adam's death, a new dimension of grief began to make its appearance: I was clearly losing the sense of my son's presence, and it terrified me. When I woke the morning after he died, I could still feel him in my space, the way a blind person senses the presence of an invisible other... But now his near palpable relevance to my world was slipping away, and I couldn't do anything about it. I wore his cross and t-shirts and haunted his old hangouts, but he continued to take evasive action. Hardly anyone talked to me about him or acknowledged his absence; it was as if he were a sensitive topic, about which the less said the better... No wonder the psalmist complained, 'I have passed out of mind like one who is dead.'
>
> Just as I was losing touch with Adam, Tracy was being blessed night after night by visions, epiphanies, and sweet dreams. In one she dreamed that Adam walked into house in the middle of the afternoon, as usual without knocking.

A few weeks later Richard was admitted to hospital for treatment; the same hospital that Adam had occupied. There he found his son.

> He did not appear to me as an apparition, but he came to me as a memory so powerful that it verged on presence... I could see the colour of his skin and feel his body, his soft hands, and the muscles in his forearms. Late into the evening and throughout the night, a great hospital makes its sounds... One of the sounds I heard on the corridor that night was the voice of my son. He called to me softly from the heart of the night and said nothing at all, as if wanting only to let me know he was there.[42]

We develop a new and changed relationship with the person who has died while learning to engage in new relationships and activities. A continuing bond can be expressed in small but significant ways. A

---

42 Lischer, *Stations of the Heart*, 221-222, 225-226.

widow described how, after saying her prayers at night, she would then always say goodnight to her husband and reach out and touch a photo of him that she kept by her bed. A man, whose grandmother died over fifty years ago, described how he expressed the continuing bond.

> Nana was a significant figure in my early years. Living in a granny flat behind our house, I would visit her most days. Her spirituality, humour, loving companionship, and gentle wisdom touched me at a profound level. Decades later, I keep her walking stick beside my bed. It's a tangible reminder of a bond that shaped a little boy – a reminder of a woman who remains a part of my life today and who I believe continues to pray for me as she did all those years ago.

For Christians, a continuing bond with the dead resonates with our belief in the communion of saints, which affirms that we are united with all God's people, living and departed. The love of God, from which neither life nor death can separate us, holds in its embrace God's children in this world and the next, and so in our fellowship with God we are united to our loved ones.

Grief Doesn't get Closed Off – so Forget about Closure

Along with 'moving on,' 'closure' tops the hit parade of clichés that are trotted out when people are facing grief and suffering. If we are to believe television reporters, closure is the magical remedy for grief. A question they frequently pose on the steps of a courthouse to a grieving family is, 'Will this sentencing / this finding bring closure to your family's distress and suffering?' It's a term strongly associated with the re-entry of the Pike River mine after an explosion killed 29 men. 'The Minister Responsible for Re-entry said, "The explosion at Pike River Mine on 19 November 2010 was a national tragedy. Today we are one step closer to finally bringing closure to the families."'

This popular notion of closure has become central for explaining what people supposedly need to find in order to heal after a loss or, as it will often be put, 'move on.' It's used to refer to finding justice, acceptance, forgetting, forgiveness, revenge, or obtaining answered questions. Yet I can find no consensus on what closure actually means. I regard it as psychobabble. What is common to many of these understandings is the idea that some action or event can bring closure or release from our grief. In other words, it will close off the grief emotions. This is a fictitious idea because it suggests that we shut off the loss, to the extent that emotions over the loss are not triggered in the future. But we never get over the loss in that it's always a part of who we are. As time passes the intensity of feelings lessens, or we might find ways to distract ourselves, or try to bury our grief-related emotions. But we aren't going to successfully close them off.

A bereaved parent found that the word closure was uttered by those who had never known the death of someone close to them and, as he put it, felt there was a subtext to the word.

> The subtext is 'It's time to move on – get over it – we've heard enough.' I think people use the word to distance themselves from grief that they are unable to deal with. Except that, for those of us who are grieving, the grief isn't closed off. Not a day goes by where I'm not affected by my loss. The loss has become a part of who I am and even though I don't choose to dwell on my grief it's got a way of sneaking in now and again. It's not because I focus on my loss and grief. It's because I loved and I lost, and it will touch me for the remainder of my days.

A father whose teenage son had been killed in a road accident said, 'I don't believe my grief will ever end. I don't want it to end. My grief is about my love for my son, and death can't destroy that love.'

Closure, like the misunderstandings about a timeline and the need to let go, poses a question: what do we choose to do with the deep emotions as they arise down the track? Their emergence isn't a sign that we haven't grieved well. They are a reminder that we can't control or predict grief. Grief works to its own schedule, and if we try to control or close it down, it will emerge at some later date with, quite possibly, unhealthy consequences. After Elizabeth's partner died of cancer, she reflected:

> The only way that I can 'handle' Grief is the same way that I 'handle' Love – by not 'handling' it. By bowing down before its power, in complete humility.

When Grief comes to visit me, it's like being visited by a tsunami. I am given just enough warning to say, 'Oh my god, this is happening RIGHT NOW,' and then I drop to the floor on my knees and let it rock me. It's a full-body experience. To resist it is to be brutalized by it. You just bow down – that's all you CAN do – and you let this thing roll through your heart and body and mind, in all its vehemence.

How do you survive the tsunami of Grief?

By being willing to experience it, without resistance. By being willing to feel everything. By being willing to accept the unacceptable.[43]

Rather than trying to forget by closing off the grief, we can remember and accept what the emotion is trying to convey.

Our Life has Changed – so Forget the idea of Returning to Normal

A common misunderstanding is that if we grieve 'normally' then we will 'get back to normal;' we will return to how we were before the loss, and our experience will not change us. This perception views grief as a temporary blip on the screen of our life. A character in one of Joanna Trollope's novels catches the reality.

Judy sat up slowly, propping herself on her arms.

'I hurt, Zoe. I hurt all over.'

Zoe looked at her, and even in the dimness of the room, Judy could see the shine of her eyes.

'It's grief again, Jude. I was thinking about it, lying there trying not to think about Joe. And I thought that one of the things about grief is change, it changes your life and the people in your life, it makes you move on when you don't want to. And that hurts. It's the change you don't want that hurts.'[44]

---

43   Elizabeth Gilbert, 7 June 2018, 'I am Willing'. Accessed from https://www.facebook.com/GilbertLiz/posts/
44   Joanna Trollope, *Next of Kin* (London: Bloomsbury, 1996), 110.

Further on I explore how grief can change us, for after an experience of significant loss we can't go back to how things were pre-loss. Our world has changed, and we must learn to live with a new normal, though it may take us some time for this new normal to emerge.

We Grieve in Our Own Way – so Forget the Stereotypes

My emphasis has been on grieving in a way that is right for you. We all differ in the ways we experience and express our grief, as well as the ways we adapt to our loss. Sometimes we will seem like a mass of contradictions: we will be with people and find that we want to escape and be alone, and if we are alone, we will wonder why no one has touched base and asked us out. Some of us will express our emotions very openly while others will be more restrained.

> Angela was worried about her husband Robert ever since their son died. Angela joined a support group. There she could openly cry and express the issues she was facing with a group of supportive parents who were going though parallel experiences. Robert didn't attend the group. Nor, it seemed, did he cry or express any deep emotion. Angela mentioned this to me, so I broached the subject with him. 'At night I go up to my son's room and I get his sports gear out. I hold it to me and smell it. Sometimes I cry. I feel close to him when I do that. I've started to keep a journal. The journal has become the place where I tell God how I really feel.'

Sigmund Freud reckoned that when we experience loss, we also experience some form of distress. He believed that if we don't display distress, that's a sign that our grieving has gone askew, and that we are denying our loss or repressing our grief. In other words, if we are to recover from our grief we need to cry and reveal some evident sign of pain. For a time, psychologists and counsellors ran with this understanding, suggesting that real grieving could only take place if we expressed our emotions in an uninhibited manner. It was the very opposite to the stiff upper lip. Repression of emotion, or reticence to express emotion, was regarded as psychologically unhealthy. The problem with this idea, like that with the stages model, is that it assumes there is one way to grieve, thus denying the uniqueness of the individual. But as demonstrated by Angela and Robert, this isn't so. We process our grief in different ways. The way we grieve, how we show our loss, isn't a measure of how much we loved the person or object that we have lost.

I suspect Freud would also have had difficulty accepting that our grief emotions are not always painful and distressing. Our experience of grief may well contain emotions such as humour, joy, and gratitude. As we think about the life of someone who has died, or a relationship or place that we have lost, we may recall times that bring us delight and thankfulness, or perhaps relief or satisfaction. Grief contains a range of emotions and all may be part of healthy grieving.

Earlier I identified how our grieving is influenced by various factors. One factor I didn't mention was gender. Literature describing grief reactions often identifies gender differences. Gender may influence how we grieve, but so do culture and temperament, family background and religious tradition. What is more, the way we grieve may well change over a lifetime. It's important not to stereotype how we grieve. For example, a pervasive misconception is that in their grieving males are less emotional and more active than females who are perceived as more emotional and reflective. This can lead to the gross misunderstanding that males feel grief less than females. It also fails to recognise that there are different understandings of what it means to be female or male, and it certainly doesn't acknowledge people who identify as non-binary or gender diverse.

I contend that it's not a matter of either / or, but a blend of influences which lead to preferences of style.

Terry Martin and Kenneth Doka[45] suggest three basic patterns of grieving:

> Heart / Intuitive grievers.
>
> Head / Instrumental grievers.
>
> Heart / Intuitive + Head / Instrumental grievers.

---

45 Terry L. Martin and Kenneth J. Doka, *Grieving Beyond Gender: Understanding the Ways Men and Women Mourn,* revised ed. (New York: Routledge, 2010) and their previous book *Men Don't Cry… Women Do: Transcending Gender Stereotypes of Grief* (Philadelphia: Brunner / Mazel, 1999).

None of these styles is better or 'righter' than others. They simply suggest a preference. We may well incorporate aspects of both and have different responses to different losses, and our preference may change over time.

Heart / Intuitive pattern:

> You tend to experience, express, and cope with your grief emotionally.
>
> You may well experience your grief in waves of different emotions.
>
> You have strong feelings of grief and it will be important for you to explore, express, and share your emotions and to know that they are valid.
>
> Especially early on, following your loss, you may find that these emotions are so strong that they inhibit your ability to focus or think straight.
>
> Your expression of grief will mirror what you are feeling inside.
>
> You may find it helpful to have a safe place, such as a support group or trusted companion, where you can express your feelings.

Head / Instrumental pattern:

> You tend to experience, express, and adapt to your grief in cognitive and physical / active ways.
>
> You do more thinking about your grief than feeling.
>
> You may well experience your grief as thoughts, such as flooding memories.
>
> You will tend to express your grief in physical ways; you will want to do – to be active.
>
> Because you need to 'do something' in response to your loss and because you are processing your grief 'in your head,' those around you may not understand, and worry that you aren't 'dealing with your grief,' when in fact you are just doing it differently.

Heart / Intuitive + Head / Instrumental pattern:
> This is a blend of the two and most of us probably fall somewhere along the continuum between heart / intuitive and head / instrumental grievers. Which means we borrow coping tools from both ends of the spectrum and we move back and forth between the two.

5 – Experiencing Grief

A popular understanding of grief, which is reflected in dictionary definitions, is that it's primarily sadness and sorrow. Grief is far more. William Shakespeare captures its complexity.

> My grief lies all within;
> And these external manners of laments
> Are merely shadows to the unseen grief
> That swells with silence in the tortured soul.
>
> (William Shakespeare, *Richard II*, IV i)

More than Sadness

Nicholas Wolterstorff describes grief as 'banging your head against the wall because you know that what you want with all your heart can't be.' Because grief is the deep need and want to have back what we can't have, it's inherently irrational. Nicholas goes on to say:

> This makes people who are not acquainted with grief want to say to a person in grief, 'get over it, shape up. You can't bring him back.' That irrationality that lies at the heart of grief is what leads many to think that the person in grief needs counselling or therapy. Granted that some need therapy. However, there is nothing irrational or pathological about grief. That is how things should be.[46]

Our profound and painful pining for what we have lost, our deep need to have back what we can't have back, is the essence of grief. Our sadness and tears, our sorrow and mourning, are expressions of our grief. They are reactions to the loss, but they aren't grief itself, nor are they necessary expressions. While it's quite possible to grieve very quietly and not shed a single tear, we tend to identify sadness and crying as the primary expression of grief and we don't identify other expressions such as irritability or anger, difficulty in concentrating, withdrawal, or physical pain as stemming from grief.

---

46 Nicholas Wolterstorff, 'Living with Grief' 1 January 2011 at Yale Divinity School. Accessed from http://www.veritas.org/living-grief/

Experiencing Grief

A significant loss can affect every facet of our being:

- body – our physical reactions
- emotions – our feelings
- cognition – our thinking and mental processes
- behaviour – our actions
- spirituality – our relationship to God and what we believe.

There are numerous well-researched studies that identify common reactions to loss, and all these experiences of grief can be regarded as 'normal'. That doesn't mean that in grief we will experience all these reactions, but if we recognise some of them in our grief, we can know that we aren't peculiar. Because we don't talk openly about loss and grief, we fail to grasp what's common in our experiences. I often find myself helping to normalise people's reactions to a loss. I've lost count of the times a person who is grieving describes a reaction, and when I tell them that it's commonplace, there's an audible sigh of relief. 'You mean I'm normal – I'm not silly – I'm not going crazy.'

In the immediate aftermath of a loss we can experience a whole range of reactions, to such a degree that it can feel overwhelming. In the early days and weeks of her daughter's death, Lucy Hone found herself experiencing confusion, anger, numbness, frustration, fear, anxiety, relief, jumpiness, sadness, and helplessness, to name just a few. There were so many of these feelings that they came together, and it was hard for her to pinpoint what she was feeling. 'Mainly numb with shock, I guess. Overwhelmed and helpless, certainly.'[47] That's how it was for Lucy, but it would be a mistake to say that raw grief, the grief we experience in the early days, looks a certain way, for we all handle our loss in different ways: head or heart; intuitive or instrumental; or both.

---

47 Hone, *What Abi Taught Us*, 6.

Grief Isolates

Before we think further about how grief affects us we need to name an underlying dynamic: grief isolates. Following his wife's death, C. S. Lewis wrote:

> An odd by product of my loss is that I'm aware of being an embarrassment to everyone I meet... I see people, as they approach me, trying to make up their minds whether they'll 'say something about it' or not... Perhaps the bereaved ought to be isolated in special settlements like lepers. To some I am worse than an embarrassment. I am a death's head. Whenever I meet a happily married pair I can feel them both thinking. 'One or other of us must someday be as he is now.'[48]

Grief makes lepers of those who grieve because it's something we would prefer to avoid. It's quite true that some people will cross the street, switch supermarket aisles, or about turn to avoid speaking to a grieving person. We recoil from suffering as if it was something contagious, and perhaps in a way it is. Being in the presence of pain awakens our own vulnerability. It reminds us that we too will lose what is precious; we also are subject to grief and one day who and what we love will be taken from us. As C. S. Lewis said, it's that 'one or other of us must some day be as he is now.'

Iris Murdoch remarked, 'The bereaved cannot communicate with the un-bereaved.' Because we have hidden grief away, because death is submerged in euphemisms, because loss and the pain it causes is something we don't want to know and talk about, a gulf has emerged between those who are grieving and those who are not grieving.

Isolation also occurs because of the uniqueness of our grief. No one else can know how we feel, and when they say they do, we know it's not true. We experience grief in such different ways. Even when we share the same loss with others, we are still alone because our grief has its own character. This was an important realisation for Nicholas Wolterstorff. Shared grief isolates the sharers from each other.

---

48 Lewis, *A Grief Observed*, 12 -13.

> The dynamics of each person's sorrow must be allowed to work themselves out without judgement. I may find it strange that you should be tearful today but dry-eyed yesterday when my tears were yesterday. But my sorrow is not your sorrow.
>
> There's something more: I must struggle so hard to regain life that I cannot reach out to you. Nor you to me. The one not grieving must touch us both. It's when people are happy that they say. 'Let's get together.'[49]

In grief, especially in the immediate experience of a significant loss, all our energy is taken up with simply surviving. Our loss dominates everything, but for those about us, our loss is an event that has come and gone. They go about their daily lives while we are trying to come to terms with a life that's been thrown into chaos; that's been turned upside down and inside out.

Disenfranchisement accentuates our grief. Alise's mother was diagnosed with motor neurone disease and died 11 months later. Her marriage of 16 years ended after she had an affair. Alise remarried, became pregnant, and then suffered a stillbirth at nearly 36 weeks of pregnancy. Her 16-year-old came out as a transgender man, and because she and her husband supported their transgender child, they were asked to leave their church. Alise felt she was drowning in grief.

Alise's experience of grief for each loss was quite different. The grief for her mother was drawn out as she lost her mother bit by bit over 11 months. Grief for her marriage was hidden. Because she had initiated the ending of the relationship, she thought she had no right to grieve. She felt her grief for her teenage child was selfish. While she was losing her daughter, she had not lost that child and he was coming into himself. This grief was compounded by anger at the injustice done to her family and the LGBTQ community. When she mentioned the loss of her stillborn son, she would often be met with uncomfortable silences and an abrupt change of subject. The message she received from her faith community indicated that it would be better for everyone if her griefs were kept under wraps.

---

49   Wolterstorff, *Lament for a Son*, 56.

Reflecting on these experiences Alise writes:

> No one said, 'You aren't allowed to grieve these losses,' but the actions and words indicated that it would be better for everyone if that grief was kept private and to a bare minimum.
>
> Rather than being encouraged to embrace grief, I was subtly told to put my grief aside and just move on. The unspoken statement was that if I spent too much time dwelling on grief, I would never be able to have a happy life.[50]

Experiencing grief and having it recognised by others are two very different things and yet they are intertwined. We need freedom to express and embrace our grief. To be denied that opportunity says, by implication, that our grief is an inappropriate thing. This only intensifies our isolation, and hearing the message that our grief is inappropriate, we quite naturally hide it away, which in turn adds to the pain. This was Alec's experience after a significant relational loss.

> It really hurt when many of my friends, and even family members, acted as if nothing had happened. They didn't even know how to say, 'I'm sorry.' I guess they thought that mentioning it to me would hurt me even more. But the worst thing a person can do is to say nothing.

People's reticence or inability to acknowledge a loss isn't generally an intentionally callous or uncaring act. Often, it's because they simply don't know what to say or are afraid of causing more pain by mentioning it. But ignoring the grief and pretending the loss never happened only accentuates the sense of isolation, and in the isolation of grief, what is needed is communication and connection.

Don't be afraid to refer to the loss or death. You will not add to the hurt, for when we grieve, we live with the painful reality of our loss every day. Failure to recognise the loss and to acknowledge the grief implies that it's something that's either insignificant or shameful, rather than a natural thing, the right thing to be experiencing. It

---

50 Alise D. Chaffins, *Embracing Grief: Leaning Into Loss to Find Life* (U.S.A., Createspace, 2015), 12.

Experiencing Grief

denies the grieving person the opportunity to share their grief and suggests that it should be hidden, which only adds to the pain.

When we are grieving, we will find there are those who are unable to give us the space and freedom to grieve. It may be necessary to remove ourselves from them, for a period at least. Then in time it may be possible to renew the relationship. We also need to be wise about who hears our story of pain. Facebook or Twitter are not always a safe forum. Seek out those who have proven themselves to be safe and trustworthy; who will listen without judgement; who will treasure your humanity and honour your vulnerability.

Experiencing Grief in our Body

Grief is physically exhausting, and it manifests in bodily reactions which can be disturbing, even frightening.

> Some days my hand would shake so much that if I picked up a pen I could barely write. My signature changed, which caused a problem or two with the bank. I remember standing at the top of the stairs and my legs would not move, and when they did I had the overwhelming feeling that I would fall. I was no longer in control of my limbs. Even when talking my mouth would feel somehow disconnected and I found it difficult to form words. Brain and voice seemed no longer synchronised. I would fall asleep at odd times.... Then I would wake in the small hours and restlessly only sleep again in brief snatches. I became accident-prone. A cup would be dropped or a glass knocked over with disturbing regularity.[51]

Grief drains us of energy. C. S. Lewis was struck by 'the laziness of grief.'

> Except for my job – where the machine seems to run on much as usual – I loathe the slightest effort. Not only writing a letter but even reading a letter is too much. Even shaving. What does it matter now whether my cheek is rough or smooth?[52]

---

51 Stephen Oliver, 'No one ever told me' in *Inside Grief,* Stephen Oliver (ed.) (London: SPCK, 2013), 6.
52 Lewis, *A Grief Observed,* 8.

The Grief Walk

When we are grieving we shouldn't be surprised if we are listless and feel constantly tired. Adjusting to momentous change is exhausting. We may find we can't sleep well or conversely we may discover we want to blot it all out and sleep all the time. Grief is stressful and we need to be in good shape to deal with it.

Common physical reactions may include:

- tiredness
- headaches and tenseness
- lack of appetite or overeating
- unexplained aches and pains
- tightness in the chest
- knots or hollowness in the stomach
- weakness of muscles
- over sensitivity to noise
- breathlessness
- lack of energy
- dry mouth
- constipation or diarrhoea
- menstrual irregularities
- change in sexual drive
- chest and / or abdominal pains.

If these reactions persist it's wise to visit your doctor, explaining your circumstances and the symptoms you are experiencing.

Experiencing Grief in our Emotions

Common emotional reactions may include:
- sadness
- anger
- guilt and regret
- anxiety
- loneliness
- inadequacy
- yearning
- hurt
- relief and peacefulness
- fear and panic
- depression
- rejection
- confusion and forgetfulness
- helplessness
- apathy
- fear and panic.

The problem with feelings is that we have to feel them, and sometimes that can be disconcerting if not downright scary. Our emotions can be messy. We may have grown up with the idea that there are positive and negative feelings; that some feelings are acceptable, and others aren't. But feelings just are. They are neither right nor wrong. The question is what we choose to do with them. Do we ignore them or face them? Do we hope that they will go away, or do we acknowledge them and find some way of expressing them in a safe, healthy, constructive manner?

Two feelings that get a particularly bad press are anger and guilt, and when they emerge, we don't know what to do with them. They leave us worried, feeling bad about ourselves because we felt them in the

The Grief Walk

first place. This adds to the pain of our grief. Pam Heaney describes the dilemma.

> Our feelings are an uncomfortable part of grief, both because we experience them intensely and because there are so many to cope with. We feel dreadful because we may begin to be angry at the person who has died, or the thing we have lost, or perhaps because we have been left to deal with the bills, or kids, or simply because we are on our own.[53]

When these feelings arise, we may find ourselves putting a lid on them. 'I shouldn't say things like that – people will think I'm not very nice. They'll think I'm a dreadful person and won't like me anymore.' Then we rationalise our feeling by blaming ourselves, because this isn't grief. Or so we think.

We may feel guilty about the things we did or wish we had done differently; about things we said or didn't say; about the way the relationship ended; about not performing as well as we should have, resulting in the loss of a job or status; that we didn't pursue our dreams with enough passion.

We need to differentiate between two forms of guilt: rational and irrational. Rational guilt is reasonable. It arises because we know we did something wrong or neglected to do something that we could have reasonably done. Irrational guilt is out of all proportion to our real involvement, responsibility and capability, and is unrelated to what we have control over. We all experience irrational guilt. It's a matter of degree, and sometimes the line between the two forms of guilt can be blurred. Rational guilt is appropriate and can prompt us to focus afresh on our relationships and priorities. It can help us make better choices in similar situations that arise. We can use our guilt as an opportunity to learn and grow. Guilt also triggers the need for forgiveness, though forgiveness usually implies our behaviour towards others. Christians readily acknowledge the need for forgiveness from God and from others, but we also need to forgive ourselves. A declaration of forgiveness used in my tradition, and

---

53 Pam Heaney, *Coming to Grief: A Survival Guide to Grief and Loss* (Dunedin: Longacre Press, 2002), 37.

which always gets to me, simply states: 'God forgives you. Forgive others; forgive yourself.'[54]

Anger is an emotion that can cause us to feel very uncomfortable and for many adds to the feeling of guilt. We worry about being rude or just appearing less than 'nice.' How will it affect others? Yet, anger is frequently an integral and legitimate aspect of our grief. Donna, who experienced several miscarriages, describes the place anger had in her grief.

> I remember my own anger feeling like balls of fire inside me that I sometimes wanted to hold and sometimes wanted to throw – at the one insensitive doctor I encountered during my hospital stay, at my husband who wasn't sharing my reactions, and sometimes at anyone who was acting like the world was still an okay place.

Our primary concern is not to decide if our anger is appropriate. What we need to do is acknowledge our feelings. As long as our expression of anger isn't hurting ourselves or others, it's not something that has to be reined in. Anger is an emotion, and like any emotion it's neither good nor bad, right nor wrong. What it's seeking is acknowledgement and expression. We need to find a safe way to express our anger. It can be helpful to verbalise our feelings or write a journal entry. We can express our anger through art or writing, by hitting a pillow, through vigorous exercising (which is a favourite of mine), or by ripping something up.

Further on we shall see how anger is given its rightful place in lament, for the ancient Hebrews understood, as we need to, that anger registers a protest about the loss that's occurred. Anger is a rightful response to an experience that's devastating, unjust and unwarranted. Anger also seeks to nurture the hope that somehow what has happened can be either reversed or put right. Anger, therefore, looks for a target, usually the perceived creator of the loss. It's also a form of control. We get angry when we feel impotent and helpless and so anger is aimed at regaining control and a sense power.

---

54 *A New Zealand Prayer Book, He Karakia Mihinare o Aotearoa*, 458.

As time goes on we need to confront the root of our anger. We need to understand what is behind it and what we are really angry about. Left unattended and unresolved it can damage us, leading to bitterness and sometimes depression. Pam Heaney explains.

> The only life it is then permitted is in substitute behaviours… which are costly, and destructive. Sarcasm, gossip, and criticism are all forms of an indirect expression of anger. They afford temporary relief by focusing on the shortcomings of someone else and help to avoid looking at their own problems. Unexpressed anger is commonly displaced into psychosomatic based illnesses, and / or depression.[55]

Loneliness is another common feeling in grief; it's an expression of the isolation that grief can cause. Loneliness can be particularly keen if someone we have been close to for a long time has died or gone away. We may miss having someone around to chat to about the ordinary stuff of life and to share everyday tasks. It can be very lonely, too, when some time has passed and those around us have got on with their lives, but we are still feeling our loss keenly. Loneliness is accentuated when the loss and grief is disenfranchised.

It's not uncommon for grief to contain relief. Sometimes it's a relief that the death or loss has finally happened; that this death that we have been worrying about for months is finally a reality that we can deal with. There's also relief that our lives are freer or less stressful now that we no longer have to care for someone. It's also normal to feel glad that a person's suffering is over, or relieved that someone we had a strained or painful relationship with is no longer around, and we can begin to rebuild our life.

It can be hard not to feel guilty about this sense of relief. We can be expected to 'put someone up on a pedestal' when they have died, but we also need to remember that like us they are human, with strengths and weaknesses.

Sometimes after a loss, when the reality of it sinks in, we may find ourselves feeling depressed and unmotivated. A loss of self-esteem

---

[55] Heaney, *Coming to Grief,* 47-48.

and a lack of direction or purpose are common, especially if we feel we are taking a long time to come to terms with the loss.

When someone dies or leaves us, we may feel rejected and abandoned. We may feel that God has abandoned us at a time when we particularly needed God's support. We may also feel rejected by the friends we thought would be most supportive, or unwelcome at social functions because of our changed situation.

It's possible that we become confused and forgetful, and getting simple, everyday tasks done is a big hurdle. It's as if our mind is filled with thoughts of what has happened, and we can't concentrate on anything else.

Experiencing Grief in our Thinking and Mental processes

Common cognitive reactions may include:

- shock
- disbelief – it didn't really happen – there must be some mistake
- confusion
- memory loss and absent-mindedness
- inability to concentrate
- impaired thinking
- depersonalisation
- preoccupation with the loss
- heightened or extraordinary experiences
- fearfulness or panic attacks.

Grief affects the way we think and perceive what's happening around us and to us. We may struggle to focus or concentrate and find it hard to organise our thoughts. Little things that were no trouble to us before can throw us, and we may worry about how we will cope. We may even have difficulty remembering the names of close friends or even the names of common objects. There can be a sense of depersonalisation, a feeling that nothing seems real and that we are simply going through the motions or operating on autopilot. David, who had had been made redundant and whose wife miscarried, all in the same week, spoke of getting into his car, driving to his destination, and on arriving having absolutely no recollection of the 40km journey. In another example, Stephen describes how at times he felt that he was losing his mind.

> I found I could not concentrate on anything. I love to read, but I could only manage a couple of paragraphs before my mind went walkabout somewhere else. I wandered aimlessly about the house, unable to rest for more than a short time. I would begin one task only to leave it unfinished and start another. Yet I had no real focus and no energy... People who left a message on my telephone asking me to ring back might just as well have asked me to run a marathon... In these earlier days those who were most helpful were friends who did not go to the trouble of asking but simply told me what I was to do. 'We are coming over for lunch and bringing a fish pie. All you need to do is open a bottle of wine!' At least it got me moving, but it was by tapping into the energy of friends, because I simply had none that I could generate for myself. At this time I depended a good deal on other people taking the initiative.[56]

It is not uncommon for people learning of a major loss to experience shock or numbness. This is a defence mechanism, which has been described as God's anaesthesia. It takes time to process the full reality of a major loss or the death of a loved one, so it's quite natural if at first, we feel little, if anything. Shock helps us through the first days and weeks after a major loss. Don't feel you have to push yourself past this. The sense of numbness will fade, although it may return from time to time. As time passes the reality of the loss will begin to sink in.

---

56   Oliver, 'No one ever told me,' in *Inside Grief*, 8.

Experiencing Grief in our Behaviour

Grief affects how we behave.

Common behavioural reactions may include:

- crying
- withdrawal
- over activity
- anger and acting-out behaviours
- disturbed eating patters
- disturbed sleeping patterns
- changed sexual needs.

Crying is an obvious behaviour, but there may be other behaviours that are not seemingly related to our loss. These may emerge from emotions a grieving person doesn't face and attend to, which they then act out in unhelpful, even destructive ways. Kenneth Doka relates the account of Akiko who experienced a 'sudden divorce.'

> Just like deaths, divorces can be sudden or chronic. Some divorces are like a chronic disease; they follow after a long period of gradual decline and discord in the relationship. Others are unexpected. Akiko was divorced after her husband abandoned her for another woman. Kiki was full of anger, lashing out at all men in the office. She was soon avoided and isolated – adding to her sense of loss and grief.[57]

There are different styles of grieving. Some of us may react by immersing ourselves in activity while others withdraw. Both reactions are valid. Some experts in grief have observed that for a time we need to conserve and withdraw. It looks to others like we are returning to 'normal' but, in reality, we are doing what we have to do to get from one day to another, which can consume all our energy, leaving us emotionally and physically depleted. When we get home,

---

57   Doka, *Grief is a Journey*, 44.

we just want to be alone with our grief. While we need these times of conservation and withdrawal, we also need time with others in order to receive support and, maybe, to share our grief. It's a matter of finding a balance for ourselves.

In addition to crying and withdrawal, we may notice a disturbance to our sleeping and eating patterns. Our sexual needs frequently change. We may want more, or less, and our sexual energy may become spasmodic or non-existent. Sexual intimacy and needs are one of the least talked about aspects of grief, yet it's an integral dimension of our experience. Sexual intimacy is lost when we lose our partner or spouse through death or separation, or disability or ill health changes their sexual function or ours.

> Alice's husband died after forty years of marriage. His death 'brought into sharp relief all of the ways our lives had been inextricably intertwined.' Gone were all the pleasures and anxieties they had shared. But it was not until some months after his death that Alice was blindsided by the realisation that the sexual intimacy they had shared was gone for good. 'This felt far more essential than things like concerts and cannoning, which were things we *did* together. This was about who we *were* together. I call this feeling "sexual bereavement," and immediately understood that this loss would not be easy to share with family and friends… I soon realised that the taboos around sexuality (especially for older people) are still strong and entrenched. We're already not supposed to talk about death in polite company. Pair that with sex, and you've got a double taboo.'[58]

For many people grief decreases sex drive. It's not uncommon to experience depression in grief, and depression suppresses our sexual drive and energy. But sometimes this can jostle alongside a deep need to be touched and to be held, what a widower described as skin hunger. The loss of physical intimacy makes a bereaved person very vulnerable. It's not necessarily the loss of sexual intimacy, though

---

58 Alice Radosh, 'Taboo times two' in Rebecca Soffer and Gabrielle Birkner, *Modern Loss: Candid Conversations About Grief. Beginners Welcome* (New York; Harper Wave, 2017), 104-105.

that may be a part of it. They may not realise they are aching to be touched and held, and it is easy for caregivers to misinterpret signals. For others, grief may increase sex drive. This can be conflicting and confusing for those who have lost a much-loved spouse or partner. But when people are numb and emotionally battered from grief, they sometimes find that sex helps them feel *something* and sexual intimacy is experienced as life affirming at a time when death and loss dominates their vista.

Experiencing Grief in our Spirituality

Death or other significant loss can and often does lead a person to seriously question their belief system. The pain of grief raises questions of a spiritual nature, which can devastate some grievers while enlivening others. The enlivened griever often poses the questions with the vigour of a prosecuting counsel. In hearing these questions, how are we to respond? The questioners don't always expect an answer, only wanting us to bear witness to the pain, anguish, and struggle that lies behind the question.

If a grieving person is unable to articulate these questions, they suffer in isolation. A gift that we can offer is the permission to voice these tough questions; to be angry with God, to question God, and to voice doubt about God. This is why the writings of C. S. Lewis and Nicholas Wolterstorff are so valuable. They make plain how grief can stretch the limits of faith.

> Go to God when your need is desperate, when all other help is vain, and what do you find? A door slammed in your face, and a sound of bolting and double bolting on the inside. After that, silence. You may as well turn away. The longer you wait, the more emphatic the silence will become.[59]

C. S. Lewis was a person of deep faith and when his wife died, he felt utterly abandoned by God. As for religion, well…

> Talk to me about the truth of religion and I'll listen gladly. Talk to me about the duty of religion and I'll listen submissively.

---

59 Lewis, *A Grief Observed*, 9.

> But don't come talking to me about the consolations of religion or I shall suspect that you don't understand.[60]

For Alise that quote from C. S. Lewis was a lifeline.

> It wasn't that I had stopped believing in God after Elliott died, but I was so angry [at God], it was hard for me to find any comfort in that belief. I would look at my life and see only the places where God was supposed to intervene and had not... Religion as consolation? No thank you. Suggesting that God was kind and loving when my son was dead felt like a lie of the most cruel kind. Words of faith felt empty, and I resented hearing them.[61]

To use religion as consolation can be unhelpful. Consolation implies an attempt to soothe, to offer solace or relief, to give explanations and answers, all of which can so easily come across as diminishment or denial of the depth and rawness of our grief.

While some people find great comfort and strength in their faith, even experiencing a renewed or strengthened relationship with God, others will struggle with their beliefs, facing doubts and disbelief, questioning what they believe.

There's a part of many of us that can't but help ask, 'Why ... why me ... why now ... why not them ... why didn't God do something ... why, why, why?' This is the all-searching question, the passionate cry of anguish that seeks meaning and purpose. As we search our spirituality to see how it can speak to the crisis of our loss and grief it may result in compounding our loss as we let go of the faith and belief we formerly knew. Some may regard this as a 'loss of faith,' though what is described by that phrase can actually mean a change or rethinking of belief, which in turn may result in a transformed faith. Whatever our spirituality or belief system, loss and grief can challenge it. It's very natural to question what we once believed in light of a loss, and for our beliefs to change.

---

60   Lewis, *A Grief Observed*, 25.
61   Chaffins, *Embracing Grief*, 96, 97.

Secondary Losses and Loss of Identity

As if the loss we are dealing with isn't enough, we will, in time, almost certainly face secondary losses. They are secondary, not just in terms of impact, but in that they are a secondary result of the primary loss, and each loss initiates its own grief. C. S. Lewis, writing as to his dead wife, tells how this was for him.

> Did you ever know, dear, how much you took away with you when you left? You have stripped me even of my past, even of the things we never shared. I was wrong to say the stump was recovering from the pain of amputation. I was deceived because it has so many ways to hurt me that I discover them only one by one.[62]

The primary loss has a snowball effect. As a person recently divorced said, 'You divide the money, the house, the books, the chattels, and even the friends.' Following the ending of the relationship, which is the primary loss, there will be changes in financial security and standard of living; loss of hopes and dreams, and for some a feeling of humiliation and stigmatisation. Friends and even family members may be lost. As with the loss of a partner or spouse through death, we may have to learn new skills, take on new or different responsibilities, roles and functions. These can range from mowing the lawns to buying birthday presents, being the breadwinner to seeing the children off to school.

A significant secondary loss is the loss of identity.

> Identity is a funny thing. The way we think of ourselves, how we define ourselves, the story we tell ourselves about who we are, all of that comes together to create our identity. And yet we don't always have a conscious awareness of our identity or even a loss of identity. It often exists in the background, like the soundtrack of a film. We aren't consciously aware of it until something changes.[63]

---

62 Lewis, *A Grief Observed*, 48.
63 'I Don't Know Who I Am Anymore: Grief and Loss of Identity'. Accessed from https://whatsyourgrief.com/dont-know-anymore-grief-loss-identity/

The Grief Walk

We were created for relationship. Relationships give meaning to life and contribute to who we are. Our relationships shape our identity and when a significant relationship is changed in a radical way, so much else in our life is affected. How we see and think of ourselves is changed. *We* is now *I*. I am no longer a spouse or partner. It's just me. So, if I'm not a spouse or partner, or a parent or sibling, or a friend, or a parishioner, or an employee, who am I? Our relational identity can also change, even within an ongoing relationship. For example, when someone becomes ill our role may shift.

> Doug and Jane have a loving relationship. Over the past couple of years Doug's health has declined. Jane is now his primary caregiver. Their love for one another is obvious, but Jane is grieving for her lost identity. 'I'm not sure I know anymore who I am. I feel as if I'm no longer Doug's wife, but his nurse. My role has changed. It seems as if I've lost the relationship we've had for all these years.'

This shift in relational identity happens at many levels.

> When the second of our parents died my brother remarked, 'You realise bro we're now orphans.' The order of our family had changed, and in time I began to value in a new way my relationship with my siblings. I was now a member of the oldest generation in my immediate family.

A similar dynamic occurs when friends or family shift. A distance may arise between previously close friends or family members, and we experience a loss of community and connection to loved ones who are still living but now far away. Similarly, when we retire, lose or leave a job, even if it's by choice, we lose a sense of occupational identity. Statements like 'I'm a nurse' or 'I'm a farmer' or 'I'm a teacher' or 'I'm a carpenter' say something very loud about how we see ourselves. We have experience, knowledge, skills, and relationships related to our occupations. When we lose that occupation who are we now? How do we see ourselves?

Our physical identity may define how we are capable of physically existing in the world. It's defined in fundamental ways, like being able to work, undertaking basic tasks around the house, playing with the children or grandchildren, going for a walk or working out at the gym, or moving free from pain. Our physical self is fundamental to much of our daily life. As I wrote this paragraph the great Scottish tennis player Andy Murray was announcing his probable retirement from the sport due to a hip injury. As he made the announcement his deep grief was manifest. Who is he when he can no longer play tennis?

Shifts which may occur in faith and spirituality impact on our identity. In whatever way we define spirituality, it's a fundamental dimension to our self-understanding and how we appreciate life. When we leave a faith community, whether it's because of a change in our spirituality and beliefs, or because we have changed address, we lose a sense of belonging as well relationships and roles that were held within the faith community.

After the death of her daughter Lucy Hone experienced what she describes as a personality change.

> Where once I was extroverted, upbeat and predominately happy, I became consumed with sadness and loss. This was all new territory for me. Coming to terms with it required adjustment and acceptance of another secondary loss: I was no longer the person I used to be. I can find myself standing at a party and realise the fun has ebbed away; all I want to do is go home and curl up in bed, the sanctuary of my grief. I'm reminded of the lamentation, 'Happiness has gone out of our lives; grief has taken the place of our dances' (Lamentations 5:15).[64]

A loss may result in the loss of the person we were before this loss occurred. This is the loss of the old 'me.' We are a changed person, a different me who will never be the same again or see the world as we once did.

Loss and grief can change us in so many ways and it may feel as if we are losing control. It can feel utterly chaotic. Hilary Smith tells of the chaos she experiences in grief.

---

64   Hone, *What Abi Taught Us*, 66.

chaos

Forgetfulness.
Times and dates mixed up
missed appointments.

Food holds no interest.
Losing weight.
Sometimes I don't eat at all
or drink too much wine
The first glass makes me forget —
the third makes me remember.

In the early hours
I lie awake
watching television,
going from frame to frame
hearing babble from the radio
like a foreign language,
reading words in a book
a jumbled alphabet.

I stare at the ceiling
and the cobweb hanging from the lampshade
waiting for the birds to sing,
the noise of traffic
the patter of children's feet in the flat above.
Sounds keeping me alive
for another day.[65]

When do we Need Professional Interventions?

Given all that we can go through as we grieve, is professional intervention appropriate? Do we need to seek medical advice and / or counselling?

Although grief can sometimes feel like a physical illness it isn't, and it's certainly not a dysfunctional or abnormal state. Grief is a normal and natural reaction to loss that we can't avoid, even though we sometimes try to sidestep or suppress it. Grief is part and parcel of being human. It's painful; it can sometimes be an overwhelming,

---

[65] Smith, *Grief's Shadowed Path*, 45.

even devastating, experience. Yet most people are relatively resilient in grief. Human beings prove, again and again, an extraordinary capacity not only to survive, but to grow through terrible experiences. After all, humans have been dealing with loss and grief for thousands of years. Grief isn't meant to be an alien force that crushes us. If we embrace our experiences of grief they help us accommodate losses so that we can continue to live creative lives. Some griefs remain with us to the day we die. But we are able to adapt to a radically changed personal world and to accommodate even the most devastating losses, and still live lives that are deeply loving and life-giving to others and to ourselves.

That said, let's remember that humans are designed to live in relationship, and our connection with others enables us to traverse this painful terrain called grief. So, leaving people entirely alone in their grief isn't a good thing. We need each other. That's the nature of community and a fundamental element of Christian life. Sensitive and compassionate support is what we need to help us get through. For a number of years, I worked in private practice as a counsellor, with a particular care for those who were grieving. It struck me that many of those who paid for my time didn't need professional counselling. Their grief could not be described in any way as complicated or chronic. They were seeking a safe relationship where they could express and explore their pain. The fact they paid for my time as a counsellor said something about our loss of community in contemporary society and the lack of understanding within faith communities around loss and grief, death and bereavement.

There are, however, times when we need professional assistance. I would strongly urge seeking professional support when grief reactions include suicidal thoughts, ideas, or actions; continued weight loss; pervasive guilt; ongoing anxiety; depression, continuing problems with sleeping, and unusual fatigue. Bereavement following the death of a child or death by suicide can be particularly complex and counselling may be appropriate.

The Grief Walk

I'm not against intervention with the use of medicine, but my caution is not to use medication as a remedy for grief. The pills we take might enable us to circumvent the pain, but it will mean we don't go through the experience. It's only by going through our grief that we can grow and find something new.

6 – What do I say? What can I do?

In this chapter I discuss some things we can do to help someone who is grieving – and a few things we should not do.

Sit Beside me on my Mourning Bench

Paul, the early Christian leader, encapsulates a good response to those who grieve: 'Rejoice with those who rejoice, weep with those who weep' (Romans 12:15). To share another's gladness is easy, but it's quite a different matter to share their grief. Yet, you may be the person they have chosen to share their pain with. You are the one, for whatever reason, they have decided to share their tears with, to voice their questions to, to express their anger to, to disclose their pain and heartbreak to. And yes, it can be scary, because there's vulnerability that comes when someone invites you into their grief, not only for them but also for you.

When someone shares their grief with us, we must face up to our own griefs and acknowledge our own pain. We have not experienced what they have, and we may wish they had chosen someone else to tell their story to. But we are the one present. They have chosen to share their grief and suffering with us. What can we do? What do we say? In a reflection, which I consider one of the wisest on the subject, Nicholas Wolterstorff asks that very question.

> Some people are gifted with words of wisdom. For such, one is profoundly grateful. There were many such for us. But not all are gifted in that way. Some blurted out strange, inapt things. That's OK too. Your words don't have to be wise. The heart that speaks is heard more than the words spoken. And if you can't think of anything at all to say, just say, 'I can't think of anything to say. But I want you to know that we are with you in your grief.'
>
> Or even, just embrace. Not even the best of words can take away the pain. What words can do is testify that there is

> more than pain in our journey on earth to a new day. Of those things that are more, the greatest is love. Express your love...
>
> But please: Don't say it's not really so bad. Because it is... If you think your task as comforter is to tell me that really, all things considered, it's not so bad, you do not sit with me in my grief but place yourself off in the distance away from me. Over there, you are of no help. What I need to hear from you is that you recognize how painful it is. I need to hear from you that you are with me in my desperation. To comfort me, you have to come close. Come sit beside me on my mourning bench...
>
> Some say nothing because they find the topic too painful for themselves. They fear they will break down. So they put on a brave face and lid their feelings – never reflecting, I suppose, that this adds new pain to the sorrow of their suffering friends. Your tears are salve on our wound, your silence is salt.
>
> And later, when you ask me how I am doing and I respond with a quick, thoughtless 'Fine' or 'OK,' stop me sometime and ask, 'No, I mean *really*.'[66]

Don't offer advice or rush in with solutions or fill the silences with easy reassurance and pat answers. Don't recite the latest piece of wisdom or glib sentimentality gleaned from Facebook or quote your favourite verses of Scripture. Listen, and listen, and listen... and then, listen some more. The Greek philosopher Epictetus said, 'You were born with two ears and one mouth for a reason – so that we can listen twice as much as we speak.' True listening is a sacred act. Marian Carter, who served as a hospice and hospital chaplain, describes it as a kind of prayer.

> For as we listen, we penetrate through the human ego and hear the Spirit of God, which dwells in the heart of everyone. Real listening is a religious experience. Often, when I have listened deeply to another, I have the same sense of awe as

---

66 Wolterstorff, *Lament for a Son*, 34, 35.

when I have entered into a holy place and communed with the heart of being itself.⁶⁷

Henri Nouwen, who through his writing laid bare much of his inner life, wrote:

> When we honestly ask ourselves which persons in our lives mean the most to us, we often find that it is those who, instead of giving much advice, solutions, or cures, have chosen rather to share our pain and touch our wounds with a gentle and tender hand. The friend who can be silent with us in a moment of despair or confusion, who can stay with us in an hour of grief and bereavement, who can tolerate not-knowing, not-curing, not-healing and face with us the reality of our powerlessness, that is a friend who cares.⁶⁸

No words can adequately express all that's happening when a person knows deep grief. In fact, there's a danger that we try to fill what we experience as an uncomfortable silence with words, which is more about our own needs than those of the person grieving. Instead, we may weep with them. We are present, sitting alongside, affirming that what they are feeling and what they are saying is okay; that it's normal and valid; that what they are experiencing truly matters. As Nicholas Wolterstorff tells it, we sit beside them on their mourning bench. It's about offering solidarity, for grief can be so very isolating, even if those who grieve have others around them.

In times of crisis and emotional turmoil most of us just want someone to be with us, to walk with us in a fellowship of suffering. Beth Slevcone, who ministers as a spiritual director, speaks of our need for travelling companions.

> A travelling companion is someone willing to sit in the darkness with us, right in the middle of those excruciating 'unanswerable whys.' Someone who has developed ways to be present and compassionate with her own dark places.

---

67 Marian Carter *Dying to Live: A Theological and Practical Workbook on Death, Dying and Bereavement* (London, SCM, 2014), 92.
68 Henri J. M. Nouwen, *Out of Solitude: Three Meditations on the Christian Life* (Notre Dame, IN: Ave Maria Press, 1976, 34.

> Someone who is willing to suffer with us. Compassion mirrored through another person awakens compassion in ourselves, and compassion always moves us to better places. It is a trustworthy pointer directing us towards home and healing.[69]

Stephen Oliver, who served as a bishop in east London, describes the people who helped him most after his wife died. He regarded them as courageous people because they stuck with him, bearing his grunts and groans and lack of chat.

> Courage, because I was sending signals that I wanted to be left alone. Courage, because they knew the risk of rejection: I did not feel anger as most would understand it, but I was intolerant of those who came too close. Courage, because these were the ones who knew that they had no easy solace to give me. Those who told me it would get easier in time, that it would get better, simply did not understand that I did not want it to get easier, and there is no way I would say even now that it gets 'better.' Such condolences I did not find helpful, for they seemed not to take seriously what H had endured or how desperate was the depth of anguish in my whole being. The ones who were most supportive were those with the courage simply to be silent when presence was important but words were not. The best were those brave people who would regularly, but not necessarily frequently, drop me a note or call on the telephone just for a few moments, simply to touch base. They were the ones who flatly refused to abandon me to my isolation. When the time came, and it was after a long time, that I finally had the energy to emerge into the world again, then it was these people who were still there, still in touch. Others had largely disappeared. For those who clearly did not understand anything, I felt on occasion that I had to put up a front, though I had little energy or desire for it... I wanted to wear a shirt with words printed on the front, 'I'm OK, thank you for asking!' But printed on the back, 'I'm hurting like hell!'[70]

---

69 Beth Allen Slevcove, *Broken Hallelujahs – Learning to Grieve the Big and Small Losses of Life* (Downers Grove, Illinois: IVP Books, 2016), 175-176.
70 Oliver, 'No one ever told me' in *Inside Grief*, 4-5.

What do I say? What can I do?

The final couple of sentences echo Nicholas' plea: to push me to be honest about how I am *really* feeling. After witnessing me go through painful times, I have a few friends who insist, when they enquire how I am, 'Give me an honest answer, not a polite one.'

Some Dos and Don'ts

People usually make statements like 'It's going to be alright.' ... 'Time will heal.' ... 'God will bless you through this,' more for the benefit of the speaker than the listener. I suspect we give way to these clichés as a means to make us feel comfortable, as a way to protect us from our fears and the pain held within the silence of grief. When I'm going through the quagmire of grief, I don't want to hear that 'everything happens for a reason' or that 'God doesn't give us more than we can handle.' I want to know there's someone who will sit with me, listen to my outbursts and respect my questions, and not utter any of those inane platitudes. I certainly don't want to be told that I'll get over it and I'll find closure. There won't be closure because this loss is part of me now. My life isn't going to be the same again. And right now, it's bloody awful (and that's putting it very nicely).

Don't downplay the grief by saying things like, 'It's really not so bad.' ... 'You'll get another chance.' ... 'You can have another child.' ... 'There's always another day.' You're relating to a person who is broken-hearted and shattered by their loss. Don't pretend it's otherwise. To say to them, 'It will be okay,' denies the fact that their lives have been radically and drastically changed.

> A parishioner looked rather stressed, so I asked her, 'How are things – and I'm not just asking a polite question.' She paused, and then told me the pain and turmoil her husband was going through... the hurt and turbulence she was experiencing. I said nothing, but took her hand and then, after a time, remarked, 'Life can be shit.' Tears came to her eyes and she replied, 'Thank you. Thank you. That's it's exactly how it is. Shit!' It seems I gave her the freedom to feel what she was feeling and to express what was real for her.

Some may ask the why questions. Allow these questions to hang in the air. Don't problem-solve by giving a neat, logical answer. If the why is directed at God, don't think you have to defend God. Just let the question stand and witness to its importance. It's okay for us not to know the answer. Jesus asked why as he hung on the cross and received no immediate answer.

Don't assume how a person's faith will speak to them. The tough questions they may pose don't necessarily mean they are having a crisis of faith. To cite Stephen Oliver's experience again:

> Frankly, you need energy to have a crisis of faith and I had no energy even for that. On the other hand, the assumptions that some people made I found very difficult. 'It must be such a comfort having your faith at times like this' was one I heard quite often, and as far as I am concerned it revealed a fundamental misunderstanding of the nature of 'faith.' For me there are many words to describe what it means to embrace 'faith,' and among them I would want to see 'challenging,' 'disturbing,' 'provocative' – but 'comforting' is not one of them… 'Faith' is not some kind of comfort blanket when times get tough. Profound human questions and deep human emotions are no easier to avoid for the person who embraces 'faith' than for anyone else. From the beginning I wrestled with the big questions of meaning and purpose… In the end I had no energy to wrestle with big questions any longer, but this is very far from saying faith was abandoned. In some curious way faith became a more embracing reality in which I was simply content to be.[71]

Pay close attention to the language that the person who is grieving is using with regard to their faith. If they find comfort in their faith, then by all means, reflect that back. But if they aren't talking about faith at that point, it might be because faith isn't helpful to them in that moment. The gift we have to offer is the gift of our presence; the gift of empathy.

Don't say you know or understand what it's like or how they are feeling, for you don't and the grieving person knows you don't. Grief is unique, because it's related to a particular loss. The most we

---

[71] Oliver, 'No one ever told me' in *Inside Grief*, 10.

can have is some glimpse as to what it may be like. There may be similarities, but grief resists generalisations. Don't recite the stages of grief and tell the person what they will go through. Each person's grief walk is a one-off.

> [A friend said to Stephen] 'There is no grief like your grief.' He did not mean that my grief was worse for me than for anyone else. He did not mean that my grief was special when put alongside that of other people. But it was a kindly acknowledgement that my grief was unique to me and that anyone who claimed to know what was going on inside me simply did not have the faintest clue... Yet from others came the unspoken but real assumption that I would 'get over it' and that life would return to normal, without their ever seeming to realise that for me there was no 'normal' any longer.[72]

Do Talk About the Loss

Talk about the loss; talk about the person who has died. After her brother died, Beth appreciated the people who said things like, 'I'm sorry your brother died.' 'I loved your brother, and I love you.' 'Let me tell you a story about your brother.' 'Will you tell me stories about your brother?' 'I will not forget your brother.' Not to mention the person who had died, or the loss the person has experienced, denies the grieving person the freedom they need to grieve.

> Those who acknowledged my loss were showing that they were prepared to put a foot, even two feet into my world. I was astonished by how many people just ignored what had happened. The problem with not acknowledging it is that it put me on mute – it denied me permission to grieve – denied me the opportunity to talk about it. Much later I asked a couple of people why they never mentioned what had happened. Their reply was along the lines of, 'I didn't want to bring it up because it would embarrass you; because

---

72 Oliver, 'No one ever told me' in *Inside Grief*, 11.

> I thought you just wanted to get on with your life.' But how could I 'just get on.' It consumed so much of my energy. It was the focus of my life and I was struggling to find a life beyond it.

At the beginning of last century Anthony Trollope addressed in one of his novels the importance of speaking about a loss. Lord Lufton is talking with Lucy whose father, Dr Robarts, had died.

Lord Lufton said: 'I remember Dr Robarts well.'

> 'Do you, indeed?' said Lucy... Nobody had yet spoken to her about her father since she had been at Framley. It had been as though the subject was a forbidden one. And how frequently is this the case? When those we love are dead, our friends dread to mention them, though to us who are bereaved no subject would be so pleasant as their names. But we rarely understand how to treat our own sorrow or those of others.[73]

Only ask a grieving person how they are if you are prepared for an honest answer, and you have the time to hear it, and then it might be best to ask, 'How is it today?' for each day will be different. Robert Delaney is a comedian and sitcom star. His young son died after a malignant tumour wrapped itself around the boy's cranial nerves. Since then Robert has set out to show people what grief really looks like. Robert is asked, 'How are you?' and the asker will add hastily. 'That's a stupid question.' 'No it isn't', he tells them:

> If you're ready to hear the answer. The answer is my heart hurts, OK? I had trouble getting out of bed today, and I cried before I got up. And then I had a cup of coffee, played with my other kids, came and said hello to my wife, and then I started to feel better. Then I got sad again. So I love the question. I tell people, I'm a balloon that is filled almost to the point of bursting, and when you bring up my dead son, it's like you've let a little out. It's like a gift.[74]

---

73   Anthony Trollope, *Framley Parsonage* (London: J. M. Dent & Sons Ltd., Everyman's Library, 1906), 104.
74   Decca Aitkenhead, 'The Magazine Interview with Rob Delaney' in *The Sunday Times Magazine,* 30 December 2018, 13.

Actions of care are all-important, but numerous people have told me how questions like 'How can I help you?' or 'Call me if there's anything I can do' are very unhelpful. As a recently widowed parishioner put it:

> This placed me in the position of having to think of what I could ask the friend to do. But I didn't know what I needed or wanted. The friends that were really helpful were those who turned up and said, 'I'll come back tomorrow and take the dog for a walk.' 'Here's your meal for tonight.'
>
> If you offer help, back it up with action. Be specific about what you are prepared to do and keep to it.

Reflecting on how people responded to her, Hilary Smith wrote:

> **rain and haddock**
>
> Some people don't know what to say.
>
> They cross the road
> or talk about the weather.
> Nothing about you.
>
> Afraid
>
> because they might hurt me
> and confront the loss that is theirs.
>
> I am willing them to speak about you
> remember you.
> Don't worry about reminding me of him
> I never forget.
>
> But they talk about the rain and the price of fish.[75]

---

75 Smith, *Grief's Shadowed Path*, 34.

The Grief Walk

This letter was posted on Facebook.[76]

Dear Friend,

Please be patient with me; I need to grieve in my own way and in my own time.

Please don't take away my grief or try to fix my pain. The best thing you can do is listen to me and let me cry on your shoulder. Don't be afraid to cry with me. Your tears will tell me how much you care.

Please forgive me if I seem insensitive to your problems. I feel depleted and drained, like an empty vessel, with nothing left to give.

Please let me express my feelings and talk about my memories. Feel free to share your own stories of my loved one with me. I need to hear them.

Please understand why I must turn a deaf ear to criticism or tired clichés. I can't handle another person telling me that time heals all wounds.

Please don't try to find the 'right' words to say to me. There's nothing you can say to take away the hurt. What I need are hugs, not words.

Please don't push me to do things I'm not ready to do or feel hurt if I seem withdrawn. This is a necessary part of my recovery.

Please don't stop calling me. You might think you're respecting my privacy, but to me it feels like abandonment. Please don't expect me to be the same as I was before. I've been through a traumatic experience and I'm a different person.

Please accept me for who I am today. Pray with me and for me. Should I falter in my own faith, let me lean on yours. In

---

76 Caleb Wilde, 'Words From a Grieving Friend'. Accessed from https://www.calebwilde.com/category/death/comforting-the-bereaved/

return for your loving support I promise that, after I've worked through my grief, I will be a more loving, caring, sensitive, and compassionate friend – because I have learned from the best.

Love,
(Your name)

It's about Relationships

Being with those who grieve is about relationship. A loss changes our personal landscape, and what usually sustains us and enables us to keep going is relationships.

We don't creatively traverse traumatic experiences alone. We need the support of others to get through tough times. A number of sophisticated studies have shown that certain types of social support are more useful to the bereaved than others. For instance, by studying the emotional wellbeing of recent widows one survey revealed that widows seeking 'emotional support' adjusted more quickly to their loss than widows seeking 'instrumental support.' In other words, in the early stages of bereavement, lending a sympathetic ear proved more helpful than mowing the grieving person's lawns.[77] It was like that for me in a time of grief. I'll always be grateful for a couple who often had me around to their home – just to hang out with them, to share a family dinner, and to allow me to talk. They shared companionship that was real. They could cope with a bloke shedding some tears without saying dumb things like, 'You'll get over it.'

Don't underestimate the value of texting as a means of supporting and being with another. I know several people who will not hesitate to send me a text or a personal message on Facebook that simply says 'Need prayer' or 'It's tough today.' They often say nothing more and I simply reply, 'I'm with you' or 'Praying.' During challenging times my wife lights a candle for me. The candle says the things for which there aren't words. It's also a visual link for me. I see the flame in my mind's eye; I see the human and divine companionship.

---

[77] Hone, *What Abi Taught Us*, 123.

soul friends

I want to be on my own
where no one will find me.

Margaret and May, Mary, Kevin and Bill,
e-mailing, consoling,
listening, holding,
comforting

Anne and Scott, Esma, David, John and Grant,
shopping, cooking,
phoning, texting,
dependable

Eva, Hilario, Dorothy, Ken, Jenny,
there

Chris, Danny, William, Murray, Jean, Yve, Odile,
sharing, sustaining, space-giving,
always in the background

Clive,
loving me, moving me on

healing voices
loving presences
gifts from God
without them …

I would not be here.[78]

Caring Companionship

We can look at caring as an attitude of the strong toward the weak, the healthy toward to the unhealthy, the powerful toward the powerless, but the original meaning of the word suggests something quite different. The word 'care' finds its roots in a very old German word, *karo*, which means to lament, to grieve, to cry out with. Care is about being with someone and entering into their pain.

To care for another isn't a matter of standing on the outside looking in. On the contrary, it's being with the person and experiencing something of their pain; being present to them in companionship.

---

78 Smith, *Grief's Shadowed Path*, 55.

What do I say? What can I do?

A resource prepared for bereavement caregivers offers what is called *The Companioning Model of Bereavement Caregiving.*

Companioning is about honouring the spirit;
it is not about focusing on the intellect.

Companioning is about curiosity;
it is not about expertise.

Companioning is about learning from others;
it is not about teaching them.

Companioning is about walking alongside;
it is not about leading.

Companioning is about being still;
it is not about frantic movement forward.

Companioning is about discovering the gifts of sacred silence;
it is not about filling every painful moment with words.

Companioning is about listening with the heart;
it is not about analysing with the head.

Companioning is about bearing witness to the struggles of others;
it is not about directing those struggles.

Companioning is about being present to another person's pain;
it is not about taking away the pain.

Companioning is about respecting disorder and confusion;
it is not about imposing order and logic.

Companioning is about going to the wilderness of the soul with another human being;
it is not about thinking you are responsible for finding the way out.[79]

---

[79] 'Grief Counselling Resource Guide: A Field Manual' (New York State Office of Mental Health, 2004). Accessed from https://omh.ny.gov/omhweb/grief/griefcounselingresourceguide.pdf

Silence, Tears, and Empathy

In conversations with people who seek to offer appropriate support to those who are grieving, questions regularly come up around three dynamics: silence, tears, and empathy.

Silence as well as speech: knowing there's a time to speak and a time to keep silence. Silence is usually interpreted as a lack of words: 'I've nothing to say,' 'Words fail me.' But silence can be more than that. Penelope Wilcock suggests this interpretation:

> Maybe silence is naked, intense communication. Perhaps words clothe the nakedness of being that is revealed in silence, so that silence forces into view the self that would rather have taken refuge in the exchange of words, the easier currency of conversation.

Sometimes it's just a question of appropriateness: learning when to use both speech and silence. Penelope goes on to say:

> Words are empty and meaningless when the companionship of silence is needed. Silence is felt as threatening or oppressive when we long for the comfort and reassurance of conversation. [80]

A space for tears: following his mother's death, Augustine of Hippo struggled with his grief. He didn't think it right to weep and moan because that's a sign, he thought, of 'total extinction.' Yet he remained 'secretly weighed down with grief.' Then, as he wrote:

> It was a comfort to me to weep for her and for myself and to offer my tears to you for her sake and for mine. The tears which I had been holding back streamed down, and I let them flow as freely as they would, making of them a pillow for my heart. On them I rested… [81]

Augustine was keen to record that his tears were strictly between him and God. It may be so for some of us. We may regard crying as

---

[80] Penelope Wilcock, *Spiritual Care of Dying and Bereaved People* (Abingdon: The Bible Reading Fellowship, 2013), 59.

[81] Saint Augustine, *Confessions* (trans. R. S. Pine-Coffin) (London: Penguin Books, 1975) IX, 12, 202.

What do I say? What can I do?

a failure of self-control and a matter of shame. Men often grow up with the maxim, 'big boys don't cry,' for tears are considered a sign of weakness, though we silently cry in the heart. The freedom to shed tears without embarrassment or apology is a gift that we can offer one who is grieving; to be a person with whom it's safe to cry; who isn't alarmed by the shedding of tears. Yet, when tears come, how often does someone say 'I'm sorry'? Perhaps we have said it ourselves. But tears are to be treasured. A line in the psalms says, 'you (God) have stored up my tears in your bottle' (58:8 *ANZPB*). It's a graphic image: God of all grief tenderly collecting and treasuring our tears. Nicholas Wolterstorff commented, 'I shall look at the world through tears. Perhaps I shall see things that dry-eyed I could not see.'[82]

On the other hand, there is no 'ought' to crying. The injunction 'You should cry' is as damaging as 'You mustn't cry.' For some, tears come gradually, and for others when we are alone. We need to find our space for our time for weeping, as we need to for other expressions of deep emotion.

Empathy: this is a challenge because when we seek to be empathetic, we need to lay 'I' aside and be totally with the other person. Penelope Wilcock expresses it aptly:

> Watching and listening with hungry intensity, I try to absorb into every surface of being and sensitivity all that emanates from the person I am with: the look on the face, the turn of the head, the laughter lines around the eyes, the little frown of stress, the brief catching breath of pain. To read the being of another person is like reading a novel – tone of voice and body language yielding a story, a mythology, an unfolding tale or map.[83]

Empathy is demanding because it requires that we make the other person our total focus for a time; that we give them the gift of our whole being. Empathy is love, compassionate love. Empathy says, I am with you. Empathy and compassion are intertwined. Compassion comes from two Latin words: *pati cum*. Combined they mean *to suffer*

---

82   Wolterstorff, *Lament for a Son*, 26.
83   Wilcock, *Spiritual Care of Dying and Bereaved People*, 80.

The Grief Walk

with. Compassion is about sharing in the pain of grief, brokenness, fear, confusion, and anguish. I think it's what Paul meant when he encouraged us to weep with those who weep.

When we learn to walk alongside a person who is grieving – not trying to remove their pain, but being present to the pain, sharing their tears and being still in the silence – we share in the birth of a very special companionship, the companionship of the broken-hearted.

7 – Grief is about Love and Attachment

After the death of her husband a woman exclaimed:

> I'm not afraid of my grief. It's not something to be swept under the carpet or hidden away. My grief speaks of my love. Why should I want to lock up my love like some fiend which must never see the light of day?

We grieve because love and grief are entwined. In this chapter I explore what that means for our grief walk.

Grief – the Price of Love

In *A Grief Observed* C. S. Lewis notes, 'bereavement is a universal and integral part of the experience of love.' Grief follows a relationship of love 'as normally as… autumn follows summer.'[84] Love and grief are inseparable. Catherine of Siena wrote, 'by the increase of love, grows grief and pain, wherefore the person that grows in love grows in grief.' There's no way to love without opening ourselves to loss. Colin Murray Parkes, an eminent psychiatrist who served on the staff of Saint Christopher's Hospice in London, described grief as part of the price of loving. Love is the deepest source of meaning and satisfaction in life. When we lose that which we love we encounter the deepest source of pain, and whatever and whomever we love, we may one day lose.

> The pain of grief is just as much part of life as the joy of love: it is perhaps the price we pay for love, the cost of commitment. To ignore this fact, or to pretend that it is not so, is to put on emotional blinkers which leave us unprepared for the losses that will inevitably occur in our own lives and unprepared to help others cope with losses in theirs.[85]

---

84   Lewis, *A Grief Observed*, 41.
85   Colin Murray Parkes and Holly G. Prigerson, *Bereavement: Studies of Grief in Adult Life* (4th ed.) (London: Penguin Books, 2010), 6.

Grief is a consequence of loving, or as Nicholas Wolterstorff remarked, 'If love was an admirable thing in your life then grief is an admirable thing in your life.'[86] This means that love is costly, and that grief is not only inevitable but also right and proper.

Love is the tie that binds one person to another over a period of time. It's a tie that takes various forms. When Lewis spoke of grief as part of the experience of love, he was referring to his marriage, though he knew that there are several expressions of love. He called them *The Four Loves*. *Storge*, which he translated 'affection,' in the Greek it has roots in such a relationship as parent for child. *Philia* is the bond between friends. *Eros* is erotic love, or as Lewis put it, 'being in love.' *Agape* is the unconditional and self-giving love exemplified in Jesus. We may have experienced each of these different forms of love, for they permeate our lives because we are relational beings, finding meaning in our connection with others.

We live our lives in relationship, perhaps with a spouse or partner, family members, friends, work colleagues, neighbours, with those in our faith community, service club, or sports team. Each relationship which contains a form of love plays a unique role in our lives, and each shapes our experience of grief. Love also finds expression in our desires and hopes; in our beliefs and spirituality; in our labours, such as our job, a responsibility in the community, or any role that utilises our talents and passions. Each is an expression of who we are, as are material items that we treasure because of the memories and relationships associated with them. Underlying each and every one of these loves is *attachment*.

Love as Attachment

We grieve when what or whom we love, what we may call the *object of attachment* or *object of love,* dies, disappears, or is diminished, impaired, destroyed, or radically changed. The more attached we are to the object of attachment or love, the greater the grief we experience when we either lose the object or expect its loss. This means that

---

86 Nicholas Wolterstorff, 'Living with Grief' 1 September 2011 at Yale Divinity School. Accessed from http://www.veritas.org/living-grief/

some losses cause more pain than others. Some losses will result in a grief experience that's relatively easy to cope with and integrate, while others will cause earth-shattering and ongoing grief. The grief we experience reflects our level of attachment; it's a measure of how valuable that person or thing was to us.

Love and grief are inseparable, as are attachments and grief. Being attached to another person, like being attached to a hope or dream, a vocation or a place, is a healthy thing. Attachments not only shape our identity; they also enable us to know passion and purpose. A healthy attachment creates a sense of security and meaning that allows us to explore life, to venture out and to take risks, and thus to gain more.

Not all agree with me about the appropriateness of attachments and grief. In the ancient world the Stoics advocated that people rid themselves of all attachments, so that they wouldn't experience grief. This idea influenced early Christianity and continues in some quarters. When a school friend of Augustine of Hippo died, he believed his grief was a sign that he had loved his friend too much, and he confessed it as a sin. When his mother died, he again struggled with this tension, but thankfully, by the end of his life Augustine had changed his view, coming to believe that love was part of God's created order. In the sixteenth century John Calvin, the Protestant reformer, did battle with the emergence of Stoicism among Christians, saying, 'there are also new Stoics, who count it depraved not only to groan and weep but also to be sad and care-ridden… Yet we have nothing to do with this iron philosophy which our Lord and Master condemned not only by his word, but also by his example.'[87] Not all Calvin's disciples heeded his wisdom, minimising funerals so as to avoid displays of mourning. This was consistent with many of the Reformers who propagated a stiff upper lip as the appropriate response in the face of death, for after all, the dead had been delivered from the miseries of this sinful world, and for those still living, it will not be long before they join the dead in a far better place.

---

[87] Cited by William C. Placher, *Mark: A Theological Commentary on the Bible* (Louisville, KY: Westminster John Knox Press, 2010), 206.

The Grief Walk

Whereas the Stoics argued that we should divest ourselves of attachments, modern culture encourages us to disown grief and fails to recognise many of the losses we experience. We deny others and ourselves the right to grieve a loss by not mentioning it or discounting its importance. This is what we are doing when we say, 'Get over it – get on with your life' or 'You should have moved on by now.' Then there are grief theories that encourage this disowning, in particular those that portray grief as a series of sequential stages, resulting in 'closure' (translated, 'You can now forget about it – that attachment and grief is no longer a part of your story – it's behind you').

I accept neither the Stoic view nor the modern view. We need to have attachments and have the grief that arises from the loss of these attachments. If we deny ourselves attachments, we deny ourselves love, and failure to grieve for an attachment is to disown our grief.

A Secure Base

This talk of attachment is rooted in *attachment theory*, which was developed by the English psychoanalyst John Bowlby. Like any theory it doesn't explain everything, nor should it be treated as an infallible dogma, but it's a helpful tool for understanding how and why we grieve. It's also rooted in an appreciation of human life that's consistent with the Christian view that we find meaning in relationship, having been created to love and be loved.

Physical death, and all the losses that precede it, separate us from those we love. Loss is inevitable but how we respond to it isn't. We may become bitter and rigid, or deeply fearful, unwilling to risk loving again. Or we may choose to open ourselves again to love. Our readiness to take such a risk presupposes a basic trust in life. Attachment theory proposes that such trust is dependent on our relationships, especially those formed in childhood. Bowlby talks of the importance of having a secure base from which to move into the world with confidence.[88]

A child who experiences early love and reliability with parents or caregiver (that is, a person who acts as comforter and protector)

---

88   John Bowlby, *A Secure Base* (New York: Basic Books, 1988).

acquires a secure attachment that allows the child to form secure relationships in later life and to face unknown or fearful situations with confidence and with an awareness of being loved and protected. Without this secure attachment, the child is disposed to separation anxiety, or may be unable to form any deep attachments at all. In adulthood this plays out in an inability, or at least a profound struggle, to face the tough stuff that life throws at us, especially significant losses.

C. S. Lewis opens *A Grief Observed* with the statement, 'No one ever told me that grief felt so like fear.'[89] From the viewpoint of attachment theory the link between grief and fear makes perfect sense. Separation from our object of attachment or love can trigger substantial anxiety and fear and when this separation is permanent the loss can shake us at the most basic level. If we have an insecure attachment history, the loss can be not only scary, but devastating, because it confirms our expectations that there is little safety and security in life.

We never outgrow attachment behaviour. Bowlby describes it as a cradle to grave dynamic as we have an ongoing need for relationships that give our lives meaning and security, comfort and protection. Although our early relationships strongly shape us, as adults we may still be able to make up for the secure base we didn't get in early life by forming relationships that provide the nurturing and reliability we need.

Bowlby doesn't allow for the possibility of developing a secure attachment beyond human relationships, a point made by Phillip Bennett, a priest and pastoral psychotherapist.

> No matter how satisfying our human attachments, they never provide us with an absolutely secure base. Consequently, separation anxiety can be more than a developmental arrest; it can signal a deep awareness of life's fragility and the inevitable separations which await us all. We *will* be separated, sooner or later, from those we love; in this sojourn on earth there is truly no abiding place.[90]

---

89   Lewis, *A Grief Observed*, 7.
90   Phillip Bennett, *Let Yourself Be Loved* (Mahwah, N. J: Paulist Press, 1997), 30.

The Grief Walk

This observation leads us towards God. Philip suggests that when God acts as the ultimate secure base, people may better negotiate loss and grief.

> Without God as our secure base, our love of others easily becomes distorted by our fear of loss; we cling to others for fear of losing them (which may, in fact, drive them away, fulfilling our worst fear). Or we may try to avoid the pain and loss by avoiding intimacy altogether... The secure base of God's love will not take away our losses, but it can help us discover an abiding Presence that sustains us even in the midst of things passing away. In letting ourselves be loved by God, we form attachment to the only One who cannot leave us.[91]

Phillip Bennett is pointing to the heart of Christian life, that is, a personal relationship with God.

While I believe it's possible for God to be our ultimate secure base and source of comfort and protection, this doesn't mean that the pain of grief is eradicated, for there is no way to short-circuit our grief. It does mean, however, that we may better traverse the grief experience, knowing a certain level of security, openness to new experiences of love, and an underlying sense of hope without being crushed by the fear that C. S. Lewis articulated. As a first century Christian expressed it, 'There is no fear in love, but perfect love casts out fear' (1 John 4:8a).

---

91 Bennett, *Let Yourself Be Loved*, 31.

8 – God and our Grief – But what Kind of God?

We imitate whatever or whoever it is we worship. Whatever else a god is, it's an embodiment of the ideals we aspire to. It's been said, God creates us in the divine image and we return the compliment and make God in our image.

Travelling the grief walk has caused me to critically review how I relate to and talk about God. What I offer in the following chapters reflects my experience. It's what resonates with me as I walk with others in pain and suffering and as I wrestle with my own experiences of loss.

Our Vulnerable God

The phrase 'Almighty God' is frequently used in public worship, but it's one that I'm somewhat ambivalent about. It's a title that doesn't seem to relate to either my own experiences of loss and grief, nor to others who are grieving and suffering. An implication that we can draw from the almightiness of God is that being all-powerful, God can do anything, fix everything, cure any sickness and, if we are to believe some preachers, bless us with material wealth. Therefore, when life goes wrong and chaos reigns, when health fails, when relationships break down, when we find ourselves unemployed and the money runs out, this image presents some significant questions. Are these experiences of loss and grief an expression of divine disapproval, even anger? Have we, in some way, failed in our relationship with God? Faced with a major loss, this view of God can lead to acute anger, bewilderment, disillusionment, and fear. If God is so almighty why hasn't God intervened? Can God be trusted as a secure base? It was a challenge I faced.

> In my early 20s I faced a vocational loss. All that I had prepared for and hoped for was seemingly taken away. A wise old priest counselled me, 'This will be like a theological depth charge.' It took me many years before I appreciated the wisdom of his words, for I wanted to hold on to an image

of an interventionist God whose almightiness would make things better. After experiencing further significant losses I discovered a very different image of God. This is a God who knows helplessness and vulnerability – who shares our grief and suffers with us. This is my secure base. It doesn't supply easy answers, and I've had to learn to live with God's silent responses, even the apparent absence of God. But this I know: in facing and owning our grief, I find not only that God can be trusted, but transforms in and through our most vulnerable and broken seasons.

Good News Stories of Vulnerability, Loss, and Grief

In the face of suffering we need to be very mindful of how we talk about God. As I sometimes struggle with the title 'almighty,' so Richard Lischer questioned the attribute 'good.'

> Believers confess that God is good; yet, like everyone else, we live with losses no one in his right mind would call 'good.'... Far from defending God's goodness, C. S. Lewis admitted, 'Sometimes it is hard not to say, "God forgive God."'[92]

Yet, the Christian faith has at its heart good news, which is what the word *gospel* means. How then can we speak of goodness in the face of grief and suffering?

Have you noticed the extent to which these narratives of good news contain accounts of loss and grief, pain and suffering? They are present in the opening chapters of Luke's Gospel. Mary, young, unmarried, and alone, learns that she is pregnant. Mary is in a socially perilous state. Her pregnancy is a scandal. Who can she share this knowledge with, which probably remains inexplicable even to her? Who will have any understanding or empathy? Mary goes in search of someone who will help and finds support in the home of her cousin Elizabeth, who welcomes her and offers her safety and sanctuary (Luke 1:39–45). Then there are a number of secondary losses: the loss of social standing, the gossip that must have surrounded her, her isolation and emotional and spiritual confusion. Disenfranchised losses and griefs

---

92   Lischer, *Stations of the Heart*, 229.

God and our Grief – But what Kind of God?

underlie these stories. As Luke continues his account, experiences of loss and grief keep emerging.

We see Mary and Joseph searching for a place to lodge and, finding no room, having to settle for meagre accommodation in a town, kilometres from home. They are homeless and lonely as they prepare for the birth of their child. They are also missing significant people from their lives: family and friends, people who would normally have been with them at a time like this. And to give birth in the first century was a precarious thing, for infant and maternal mortality rates were perilously high. A New Zealand Christmas carol captures the essence of this state.

> Born among the poor on a stable floor
> cold and raw, you knew our hunger
> weep our tears and cry our anger.[93]

Here is God in Jesus, as the most vulnerable of all in society: a baby crying for milk, dependent on others in all things. The story continues: when Joseph and Mary present Jesus in the temple, an old man warns Mary, 'a sword will pierce your own soul too' (Luke 2:35). What grief did she experience as she pondered these words? What would become of her son?

Matthew concludes his infancy narrative with the family having to flee for their lives and taking refuge in Egypt (2:13–14), experiencing the multiple and traumatic losses experienced by those who are refugees in any century or culture. Then Herod, seeing he had been tricked, ordered the death of male children age two and under in and around Jerusalem.

> Then was fulfilled what had been spoken through the prophet Jeremiah:
>
> 'A voice was heard in Ramah, wailing and loud lamentation,
> Rachel weeping for her children;
> she refused to be consoled, because they are no more.'
> (2:17b–18)

---

[93] Shirley Murray, 'Child of joy and peace' in *Carol our Christmas: A book of New Zealand Carols* (Raumati Beach: New Zealand Hymn Book Trust, 1996), #9.

The Grief Walk

In some traditions this massacre is commemorated as the Feast of the Holy Innocents, normally held three days after Christmas. The birth of Jesus was accompanied by violence and death, lamentation and grief. It's into this world, a world that entails loss and grief, suffering and distress, that the Son of God is born.

We then encounter the adult Jesus, reliant on others for a bed to sleep in, a roof over his head, and a meal to sate his hunger. At the end, he has a price on his head, vulnerable to the whims of those who would betray him. Then comes the ultimate demonstration of utter helplessness and vulnerability as Jesus is arrested, scourged, mocked, killed, and finally, as a corpse, laid out in a borrowed tomb.

If the crucifixion of Jesus means anything beyond an historical event, it's that God isn't outside the realities of this life, but inside at the very centre of it all, encompassing our vulnerability and helplessness, our loss and grief, our pain and heartbreak. Here is God sharing our grief walk, being abused with us, being mocked with us, suffering with us, and dying with us. It is, as the English mystic Julian of Norwich saw in one of her visions, 'a great Oneing betwixt Christ and us.'[94]

Mark the Gospel writer tells of how, in the time before his arrest:

> Jesus took with him Peter and James and John, and began to be distressed and agitated. And he said to them, 'I am deeply grieved, even to death; remain here, and keep awake.' And going a little farther, he threw himself on the ground and prayed that, if it were possible, the hour might pass from him. He said, 'Abba, Father, for you all things are possible; remove this cup from me; yet, not what I want, but what you want.' (14:33–36)

The English translation understates the force of the Greek. Jesus shudders in distress, in anguish, in horror.

> It is the picture of a man right on the edge of complete emotional collapse… This was not the ancient ideal of how a hero should face his death. A calm Socrates drank poison

---

[94] Julian of Norwich, chapter xviii, *Revelations of Divine Love* (Christian Classics Ethereal Library). Accessed from
https://ccel.org/ccel/julian/revelations/revelations.ix.iii.html

God and our Grief – But what Kind of God?

and continued to chat with his friends… Celsus, the great second-century critic of Christianity, asked how Christians could view as divine this Jesus, who mourned and lamented and prayed to escape the fear of death.[95]

This is God-with-us participating in the full compass of human experience. In the face of suffering and pain, it's not the all-powerful God that we meet. Dietrich Bonhoeffer, theologian and pastor who was executed by the Nazis in 1945 and is now honoured as a modern-day martyr, wrote to a friend from prison on the vulnerability of God.

> God allows himself to be pushed out of the world on to the cross. God is weak and powerless in the world, and that is exactly the way, the only way, in which he is with us and helps us. Matthew 8:17 makes it crystal clear that it is not by virtue of his omnipotence Christ helps us, but by his weakness and suffering.
>
> Here is the decisive difference between Christianity and all religions. [Our] religiosity makes [us] look in [our] distress to the power of God in the world; God is the *Deus ex machina* [a god from a machine]. The Bible however directs us to the powerlessness and suffering of God, only the suffering God can help.[96]

Elie Wiesel, a survivor of Auschwitz, asked that most searching question, 'Where is God?' He gave a response in his book *Night*, in which he recounts the hanging of a young child in front of the entire death camp. The boy was 'too light to break his own neck.'

> 'Where is God? Where is He?'… For more than half an hour he stayed there, struggling between life and death, dying in slow agony under our eyes… He was still alive when I passed in front of him. His tongue was still red, his eyes were not yet glazed. Behind me, I heard [a] man asking: 'Where is God now?' And I heard a voice within me answer him: 'Where is He? Here He is – He is hanging here on this gallows.'[97]

---

95 Placher, *Mark: A Theological Commentary on the Bible*, 206.
96 Dietrich Bonhoeffer, *Letters and Papers from Prison* (London: SCM Press, 1965), 122.
97 Elie Wiesel, *Night* (New York: Bantam Books, 1982), 75-76.

The Grief Walk

The good news is that in Jesus, God is one with us in our losing and grieving.

Becoming Vulnerable – Becoming like God

When we worship God, we reflect who we believe God is. If, then, God is vulnerable, suffering with us, sharing in and fully knowing our grief, then our sorrows need not be buried, but are to be shared with God and with those who journey with us. To grieve is to become like Jesus, to become like God who is vulnerable.

Vulnerability, which equates to powerlessness and helplessness, is so very different from almightiness. It isn't a state that we normally aspire to and it would seem to be out of keeping with the image of God as almighty. When faced with the vulnerability and helplessness of others, we tend either to resist or, at least, to negate it. Penelope Wilcock, who ministered as a hospice and hospital chaplain, describes this response.

> Our counsel often instinctively combats helplessness. 'Don't cry;' 'Be brave;' 'Be strong.' Likewise we sometimes respond to the helplessness of others by taking rescue action, seeing ourselves as the cavalry coming over the hill. And when we cannot make everything better, our own helplessness plunges us into shame.[98]

If we are able to accept our own sense of vulnerability and helplessness this acceptance becomes a gift to those who are vulnerable and helpless. Being at peace with our own inadequacy permits others to accept it within themselves. It enables us to be with others as they grieve; to be instruments of healing and compassion, wounded healers who have discovered within our own wounds a source of compassionate love, empathy, and wisdom from which we can draw as we walk with others in their suffering.

Suffering Love that is *With* Us

In the presence of loss and grief I gravitate towards two images for God. Matthew articulates the first. An angel tells Joseph that Jesus

---

98 Wilcock, *Spiritual Care of Dying and Bereaved People*, 14.

God and our Grief – But what Kind of God?

will be named 'Emmanuel,' which means, 'God is with us' (1:23). Matthew ends his Gospel with that same image as Jesus says, 'And remember, I am with you always, to the end of the age' (28:20). This is God who shares our suffering, who journeys with us in our grief and pain. The all-powerful and almighty God becomes the all-powerless and all-vulnerable God. This is God who, in the other image I draw on, 'is love' (1 John 4:8). To quote Penelope Wilcock again:

> There is no love without helplessness, no love without need, no love that does not yearn for an answering love. Helplessness, yearning, need; these belong inescapably to the nature of love – and God is love.[99]

Christianity proclaims the central tenets of belief within the context of God's helplessness and vulnerability in Jesus. Divine power is the power of a love that is willing to be utterly vulnerable and one with us in our helplessness. Hence, my praying tends to be focused on God-with-us; God who is love; God as vulnerable and God who knows what it is to be us.

To speak of God's love to those in deep pain can be risky. It can very easily sound like a platitude and begs the retort, 'Where is God's love in my suffering? If God is all-loving why did this happen to me?' At this point I need to say that love within the Christian context is not to be confused with how people frequently utilise the word. Love, as spoken of within Christianity, is inseparable from suffering. God's love for us is suffering love. This is what we see in Jesus. 'How else can we understand,' asks Richard Rohr, 'the revelation of the cross? Why else would the central Christian logo be a naked, bleeding, suffering divine-human being?'[100] Because God is love, God suffers. Nicholas Wolterstorff writes:

> God so suffered for the world that he gave up his only Son to suffering. The one who does not see God's suffering does not see his love. God is suffering love. So suffering is down at the centre of things, deep down where the meaning is... The tears of God are the meaning of history.

---

99 Wilcock, *Spiritual Care of Dying and Bereaved People*, 17.
100 Richard Rohr, *A Spring Within Us: A Book of Daily Meditations*, (CAC Publishing: 2016), 120.

The Grief Walk

God's suffering love forms the kernel of the life of God's people; it's the heart of what it is to be church. But a question hangs in the air, one that Nicholas goes on to articulate.

> Why isn't Love-*with-out*-suffering the meaning of things? Why is *suffering*-Love the meaning? Why does God endure suffering? Why does God not at once relieve his agony by relieving ours?[101]

A mystery remains, but what I can say is that God and we are in it together. In his next entry Nicholas writes:

> The history of our world is the history of our suffering together. Every act of evil extracts a tear from God, every plunge into anguish extracts a sob from God. But also the history of our world is the history of our deliverance together. God's work to release himself from his suffering is his work to deliver the world from its agony; our struggle for joy and justice is our struggle to relieve God's sorrow.[102]

If God is suffering love, if God knows our sorrows and our joys, it means that God knows our sense of utter helplessness and vulnerability in the face of loss. If that is so, then it really is okay for us to grieve, okay to weep, okay to be vulnerable, for when we do so, we are being who we were made to be, reflecting the divine nature, being in the image and likeness of God (see Genesis 1:26, 27). This is what we witness in the grieving and the protest and the lament of Job; the Psalmist; the women who like Rachel, wept for their children; and Jesus in the garden before his death. Each cries out the anguish of their grieving.

> You may cry out to God – and against God – from the edge of hell, when meanings unravel, when relationships break, when chaos seems lord, when God seems absent. And when and if you do, may you also know the gospel that God does not neglect such a cry. May you also know that Christ weeps in your tears.[103]

---

101 Wolterstorff, *Lament for a Son*, 90.
102 Wolterstorff, *Lament for a Son*, 91.
103 Allen Verhey, *Reading the Bible in the Strange World of Medicine* (Grand Rapids, MI: Eerdmans Publishing, 2003), 122.

Much of Christian thought around the suffering and death of Jesus focuses on what God does *for* us through Jesus. But being with those who are grieving and suffering leads me to focus on how God is *with* us through Jesus. Jesus suffered *with* us, *with* flawed and sinful people, *with* the world, *with* me, and *with* you. In Jesus, God the creator, became *one with us* in our suffering, dying, and death. As a colleague of mine remarked, 'If I had to put my understanding of Christianity into one word it would be *with*.'

There's a considerable difference between the two words: *for* and *with*, as Diana Butler Bass explains.

> *For* is a preposition of distance, a word that indicates exchange or favour, it implies function or purpose. I do something *for* you; you do something *for* me. Notice: someone does something on behalf of or in another's place. *For* is a contract. Jesus suffered *for* us – means that Jesus did something on our behalf, he acted on behalf of a purpose, in place of someone else. *For* always separates the actor and recipient, distancing a sacrificial Jesus from those for whom he died. At the cross, Jesus is the subject; we are objects.

In contrast, *with* is a preposition of relationship. *With* implies that both Jesus and we are sharing in something.

> *With* is the preposition of empathy... of being on the same side, of close association. 'No, you needn't go *for* me; I'll go *with* you.' *With* is about joining in, being together.[104]

We are not alone in what we go through. But the story doesn't end there. If God is with us in Jesus Christ, then Christians are called to be *with* others. If God is willing to walk *with* us, and suffer *with* us, then that becomes our call as Jesus-followers. We are called to do the same and to be with those around us. This isn't easy, for it calls us to share in suffering-love, and when we do, we share with another the suffering and compassionate love of the One who is Love. What we have to offer is not hollow optimism but the gift of solidarity; being

---

104 Diana Butler Bass, 'Good Friday: Being With Jesus at the Cross.' Accessed from: https://www.patheos.com/blogs/dianabutlerbass/2012/04/good-friday-being-with-jesus-at-the-cross/

with those who suffer; walking alongside the grieving person. It's the living statement: you shall not be left alone as you grieve.

Discarding the Great Vacuum Cleaner in the Sky

The image of God as being with us runs contrary to some popular religious notions and certainly challenges the tendency to offer slick platitudes.

Deep grief plunges us into an alien world. We have to learn a new reality for the world we have known no longer exists. We have lost who or what we love. What gave meaning to our lives has either been radically changed or taken from us. Questions may abound: 'Why me? How could God let this happen? What will come of me?' This new terrain can be a frightening place. Faced with the unknown we seek answers and security. Popular forms of spirituality offer ready-made solutions. One such answer was posted on Facebook: 'God won't give you more than you can handle.' I shall be frank. This response is spiritual and pastoral nonsense. Try telling that to the person who knows the intense pain of loss and grief. I know why people say it. It's an attempt to offer comfort and encouragement because it's hard to watch someone hurting, and even harder knowing there's nothing we can do to lessen their suffering.

There are several problems with this particular cliché. For a start, it's not in the Scriptures. There's a statement that sounds vaguely like it: 'God is faithful, and he will not let you be tested beyond your strength, but with the testing he will also provide the way out so that you may be able to endure it' (1 Corinthians 10:13b). Paul is talking about temptation, not suffering. His point is that God will not place us in a situation where a temptation to do wrong is irresistible but will always show us a way out. It reminds us that we aren't locked into making a sinful decision. It has nothing to do with suffering and grief.

Another problem with this statement is that it implies that God 'gives us' the suffering: that God caused the death of our loved one, the loss of our job, the life-threatening illness, the miscarriage, the loss of home and all our possessions, or the disability that we must live with.

To say this to a person who is grieving is to tell them in the midst of their pain that the very experience that they are struggling through that leaves them wondering if they will survive another day, is a gift from God. Instead of being the One who is Love, God becomes the bestower of pain and sorrow. It makes God out to be a sadist.

Like such euphemisms as 'God took her' or 'It was God's will' these statements portray God as a celestial body snatcher, or as it was put to me 'the great vacuum cleaner in the sky which sucks people up off the earth.' If this is how God behaves, it's no wonder that some bereaved people reject God out of anger and resentment.

Besides implying that God gave us these losses and griefs, this statement is usually uttered when a person is feeling that they can't handle more because they are saturated with grief. The statement invalidates them at the very time when what they need most is to have their pain recognised and honoured. As one person expressed it, 'This platitude always made me feel so weak and ashamed when I wasn't handling things. I couldn't understand why God would be putting me through pain.' Another summarised the damage it can do.

> When you're feeling suicidal that statement makes absolutely no sense and just dumps on more and more layers of failure as you feel you can't handle it. It doesn't bring God closer but more out of reach as if you've missed the magic 'stop this shit happening' button that God made. But God isn't like that at all but is the only presence in the darkest corner especially when you are past 'handling' it.

If the intention is to encourage a person to find inner strength and to remind them that they are strong, then by all means encourage them. Perhaps help them recall times in the past when you witnessed that strength within them. But please, don't tell them 'God won't give you more than you can handle.'

The only God that makes sense to me in the face of suffering and grief is the God who is prepared to suffer *with* us, to grieve and weep *with* us, who journeys *with* us in the darkness of our grief. I guess that is why this short verse speaks so loudly to me: 'Jesus began to weep' (John 11:35).

We need to think carefully about some of the things we say in the face of death and bereavement, loss and grief. What do they say about how we see God? They may be well meant but, as Hilary Smith suggests, they may also be 'one of the sins of religion / compounding confusion, doubt, disbelief.'

platitudes

> *God has taken him to heaven*
> *Your loved one has gone to a better place*
> *He's at peace now*
> *There's no more pain or suffering for him*
> *God always takes the best*
> *It's God's will*
> *When your number's up.*

If God has taken you to heaven
where is that?
A place above the sky?
A state of blessedness?
Here?
There?

If God's will takes away the best
Reaches down to take away the ones we love
to make them suffer
or let children die,
what kind of God is this?

When your number's up
What does that mean?
That names and numbers are written in a book
and when it's your day to die
that's it?

What kind of moral accountancy is this?
Don't people die for different reasons –

   accidents
   faulty genes
   age
   injustice
   war
   being in the wrong place at the wrong time?

Nothing to do with God.

Why does religion perpetuate such myths?
Fire insurance?
Control?
Rationalising mystery?

Patronising
empty apologetics
for the causes and devastation of death
may be well meant
or one of the sins of religion
compounding confusion, doubt, disbelief.

Spacious mystery is what I need to ponder
tenderness what I need to feel
arms around me to reassure.
A quiet prayer because I can't pray
or no words at all.[105]

Jesus Began to Weep

In his Gospel John tells of how Jesus' friend Lazarus fell ill (11:1ff). Lazarus' sisters, Mary and Martha, sent for Jesus, in the hope that Jesus would heal their brother. This was not an unreasonable expectation. They were, after all, three of Jesus' best friends. But Jesus waits two whole days, and then he travels a day or two more, so that by the time he arrives he has missed Lazarus' funeral by four days. John says that Jesus knew what he was doing, knowing that what would follow will glorify God. Jesus' confidence is wasted on Martha. 'Lord, if you had been here, my brother would not have

---

105 Smith, *Grief's Shadowed Path*, 42-43.

died' (11:21). Helpless and hopeless is how Mary and Martha felt when their brother died and they pose the question that we may well ask, and which John states three times (11:32, 37). 'Couldn't God do something about this? Why did God let this happen?'

Jesus didn't answer their question. He instead revealed God's nature. Profound truths can be captured in very simple statements, none more so than John's description of Jesus' response to Lazarus' death: 'Jesus began to weep.' Jesus grieved for his dead friend and entered the grief of those about him. When he saw them weeping 'he was greatly disturbed in spirit and deeply moved' (11:33).

Here is Jesus, 'the Word made flesh' (1:1–14), through whom the universe was created, sharing our human vulnerability, grieving for his friend. Here we witness God's heart wrung with the anguish of suffering, sharing our experience of grief. Here is the man of sorrows, acquainted with our grief and pain (see Isaiah 53:4).

When I'm caught with tears in my eyes, I feel vulnerable and weak because the tears are a sign of the grief and pain within. That's what we see in Jesus. Yet, he never apologised for his weeping, as I'm given to do. Here he is, unashamed of his vulnerability; revealing God's unashamed vulnerability. The vulnerable God is the God who, rather than taking our pains away, first chooses to share them with us, to enter them, and to become fully part of them. This is what we mean by the incarnation: God sharing in our human condition, suffering it, experiencing it, and dying in it.

As part of this story, Jesus goes on to say, 'I am the resurrection and the life. Those who believe in me, even though they die, will live, and everyone who lives and believes in me will never die. Do you believe this?' (11:25–26) These familiar words are frequently recited at Christian funerals, though what might they mean for a person living in the wake of the death of a loved one? It's a mistake to rush on to the conclusion of the story, ignoring God weeping with us, and focusing solely on the promise of resurrection. Grief and hope can be uttered in the same breath.

Jesus' promise, that he is the 'the resurrection and the life,' is as much for now as for the future. Martha's assumption was that the resurrection was for some future date: 'I know that he will rise again in the resurrection on the last day' (11:24). But Jesus saw that it could be something for the present. Barbara Brown Taylor offers a helpful interpretation.

> I want to use the other word for the Greek word *pisteuo*, which can mean either 'trust' or 'believe.' 'I am the resurrection and the life,' Jesus says. 'Those who trust in me, even though they die, will live, and everyone who lives and trusts in me will never die. Do you trust this?'

This promise is not about a future reward beyond this life but a present reality that we can begin living now. As Barbara puts it:

> Those who hook up with him will never die, no matter what happens to their bodies, because he is hooked up with the source and sustainer of all life. Those who trust that with him – in him – begin their eternal life right now, and nothing on earth can snuff them out.[106]

I believe in the promise of resurrection in the face of death, as I do in the face of any loss. The shape and form of that resurrection is beside the point. It's the truth in it we are given to trust. That truth is that God's love, shown to us in the shape of Jesus, is tough, persistent, and everlasting. I can believe that, or rather, I trust that, because I see God accepting our cries from the depths, weeping with us, travelling with us through the present circumstances and, ultimately, bringing us to a new place.

Before exploring what that truth might mean, we need to name our loss. We need to enter grief and give it voice. To do otherwise, by skipping forward to the hope of Easter Day and proclaiming the hope of new life, which Christians are sometimes apt to do, is to deny the reality we are living with. And psychology supplies ample evidence as to the damage that can cause.

---

[106] Barbara Brown Taylor, *God in Pain: Teaching Sermons on Suffering* (Nashville: Abingdon Press, 1998), 68.

9 – Words for our Grief – A Gift from the Psalms

> What! man; ne'er pull your hat upon your brows;
> Give sorrow words: the grief that does not speak
> Whispers the o'er-fraught heart and bids it break.
>
> (William Shakespeare, *Macbeth*, IV iii)

Grief can be so powerful and suffering so overwhelming that it seems no words will suffice. Yet we seek to give sorrow words and allow the grief to speak, otherwise the heart will break. How can we do this in a culture where grief is hushed up? At many funerals we celebrate the life lived, and rightly so, but we dare not grieve the death of one we love. Are we afraid to face the reality of our mortality, afraid to acknowledge the pain of our grief, afraid to name the depth of our loss? If we are, it's not surprising. Our culture encourages us to tuck our grief away and to move on into that mysterious state called closure.

When we gather to worship as a faith community, what do we do with the grief that we live with? What place does it have in our relationship with God, with those about us, and with ourselves? What happens after a young person in the congregation is diagnosed with a terminal illness? Or when a church leader is revealed as an abuser? Or when an earthquake, virus, or a flood wreaks havoc? What words do we use? How do we acknowledge the grief that lurks beneath the surface of any community at any time? Do we trot out the usual hymns and songs of praise and maintain a bright façade in the face of all that we are feeling? Very often, that's exactly what we do, but we need to tend to our grief and give it words. Injustices cry out to be identified, losses to be named, suffering and hurt to be expressed.

It seems to me that by and large the church has bought into this denial of loss and death and colluded with the silencing of grief. Listen to our hymns and songs. Most express praise and joy, triumph and victory. Few speak of sorrow and grief, pain and suffering. And many who know the pain of grief have, at some point, been the recipients of trite religious clichés, all of which perpetuate the denial. 'God wants to make you stronger through this.' ... 'God never gives you more than you can handle.' ... 'Everything happens for a reason.' ... 'It's all part of God's plan.' ... 'It was just their time to go.' ... 'They're in a better place.' These pious platitudes deny the pain of loss and stifle our grief. They are twenty-first-century forms of Stoicism and say, in effect, 'Keep your grief to yourself. Put on your mask and pretend everything is fine.'

Grief can be horrid, and we may want to use language that some find unacceptable. We may ask questions that are tough and unsettling and make statements that sound unreasonable and contrary to accepted beliefs. That's the nature of grief. It contains raw, unsanitised emotions. This poses a problem for many of us because we were taught to talk nicely, especially in church; otherwise we got out mouths washed out. So we got into the habit of being nice in front of others and before God. But when we turn to the Hebrew Scriptures we find something quite different. We witness people of faith giving full vent to their emotions, expressing the depth of their grief, hurling their accusations at God, telling out their anger and abandonment, voicing their confusion and complaint. The Scriptures teach us how to speak what we have to say. They utter what we have been taught not to say; what our religious culture, ironically, often prohibits us from saying. In the face of a cultural denial Scripture gives us a path to own our grief, and a language to express it within the context of Christian spirituality. We find that path in lament.

David's Dirge

The Concise Oxford Dictionary defines lament as 'a passionate expression of grief or sorrow.' It's not a restrained or mild expression, but an intensely and deeply felt expression that may well involve crying, moaning and groaning, wailing and sobbing. This understanding of lament finds poignant expression on the lips of David at the death of Jonathan and Saul. On hearing of their deaths, 'David intoned this lamentation over Saul and his son Jonathan' (2 Samuel 1:17).

> Your glory, O Israel, lies slain upon your high places!
> How the mighty have fallen!...

The Grief Walk

> Saul and Jonathan, beloved and lovely!
>   In life and in death they were not divided;
>
> They were swifter than eagles,
>   they were stronger than lions…
>
> How the mighty have fallen in the midst of the battle!
> Jonathan lies slain upon your high places.
> I am distressed for you, my brother Jonathan;
> greatly beloved were you to me;
>
>   your love to me was wonderful,
>   passing the love of women.
>
> (2 Samuel 1:19, 23, 25–26)

David loved Jonathan dearly and immensely, as he had loved no one else. Such was the love between these men that Jonathan surrendered his claim to the throne. Then there was Jonathan's father, King Saul, who tried more than once to have David killed. For both these men David grieves: his beloved friend and the man who became his enemy.

In his grief David knows a myriad of feelings. Painful though they are, he refuses to evade them. He faces his grief, and from its depths flows his song. His words for Jonathan are understandable, but what of those for Saul? They are words of honour and respect, of forgiveness and love; all for a man who had turned on him and spent years trying to have him killed. Was David in denial? Had he forgotten that Saul had wanted him dead? I don't think so. Grief is loaded with ambiguities and contradictions. One moment we are thankful and full of loving memories, the next, we experience resentment and hurt. Grief isn't a simple, clear-cut experience. David refuses to run away from his grief. He remains with it and plumbs its depths.

David's song is an outpouring of deep emotion. He gives his grief words, but there isn't as yet, a place for God. While a number of translations refer to it as a lament it's better described as an elegy or dirge, which is essentially a sung eulogy, and we need more than this.

We need a path that involves God and helps us find hope. For this we turn to biblical lament.

In David's dirge the focus is on what has been, on what has been lost. This is called the tragic reversal. Glory becomes shame, strength becomes powerlessness: 'How the mighty have fallen!' Once 'they were swifter than eagles, they were stronger than lions,' but no more. In biblical lament suffering finds a voice addressed to God. It takes the suffering, grieving person on a journey towards hope and reverses the reversal.

> Looking heavenward, lament moves from distress towards wholeness, from powerlessness to the certainty of a hearing, from anger towards confidence in God's justice, from guilt toward the assurance of God's forgiveness. The distress and powerlessness and anger and guilt are still there, still finding voice, but the very form of the lament moves sufferers toward their share in Israel's faith that a saving reversal – and not the tragic reversal – is the pattern of their existence. Attention to God allows the pattern to change, but it does not disallow the sorrow.[107]

The Voice of Lament

> Be gracious to me, O Lord, for I am in distress;
>   my eye wastes away from grief,
>   my soul and body also.
>
> For my life is spent with sorrow,
>   and my years with sighing;
>
> my strength fails because of my misery,
>   and my bones waste away.
>
> (Psalm 31:9–10)

Lament appears in various places within Scripture, but particularly in the psalms. Of the 150 psalms more than a third are psalms of

---

107 Allen Verhey, *The Christian Art of Dying: Learning from Jesus* (Grand Rapids, Michigan: William B. Eerdmans Publishing, 2011), 314.

lament.[108] These ancient poems and songs tackle reality head-on. They are a response to experiences like loss and grief, struggle and alienation, pain, suffering, and injustice. They voice the questions we have when we can't make sense of what happens to us in life. They speak out of the human heart and voice the anguish of communities and individuals. Laments are what Beth Allen Slevcove calls, 'the prayers offered after the chair has been pulled out from under the people of God.' That's why they are loaded with tough questions: 'Where are you, God?' 'Why aren't you protecting and providing for us?'

> They are, as Walter Brueggemann so helpfully puts it, the Psalms of Disorientation. Aren't we God's chosen people? Didn't God say he would protect us, and lead us through the wilderness, and care for our every need? Their expectations about God, themselves and the world have been shattered, their understandings of God forever altered.[109]

These psalms are saturated in the raw emotions that we experience when the world we know has ended, when our sense of security and safety has been ripped away and replaced by disorientation and chaos. I first took notice of the lament psalms when I was going through burn out. My ministry as a parish priest was disintegrating. It seemed that I was losing the vocation I thought I had been called to. Depression held me in its grip and the spirituality I had embraced supplied no means to express the dark emotions that tormented me. I felt excluded from the life and worship of the church where it seemed only praise and nice positive emotions were acceptable. But in these psalms, I found a way to pray in the dark.

The faith of ancient Israel allowed for the expression not only of praise, joy and thanksgiving, but also of grief, doubt, fear, and anger. As well as acknowledging the reality of these deep emotions, it gave them religious and social sanction. The community of faith

---

[108] The following are often counted among the psalms of disorientation and lament: 3, 5, 6, 7, 10, 13, 14, 16, 17, 22, 25, 26, 27:7–14, 28, 31, 35, 36, 38, 39, 40:12 –17, 41, 42-43, 51, 52, 53, 54, 55, 56, 57, 58, 59, 61, 63, 64, 69, 71, 77, 86, 88, 90, 94, 102, 109, 120, 123, 126, 129, 130, 140, 141, 142, and 143.
[109] Slevcove, *Broken Hallelujahs*, 64.

provided the suffering person a voice, and lament supplied not only a vocabulary but also a sense of direction. Richard Lischer's son Adam was dying with cancer and Adam's wife Jenny was pregnant with their first child. Adam told Richard that he and Jenny prayed the psalms most nights.

> I understand why. The psalms are filled with the complexity of rage, and so was Adam. It is never pure anger at work in any of us, and it wasn't in him, but anger in the disguises and permutations of fear, suffering, sadness, and bafflement. The psalms are filled with questions; they ask 'why?' and 'how long?' Sometimes they address God disrespectfully in a manner that good religious people find offensive. But they also offer more than the usual, therapeutic alternatives of suppressing the rage or projecting it onto others. They invite the believer to lay the whole mess before God. The psalms treat God as a partner in suffering and in doing so they open a narrow path from lament to a grudging acknowledgment of God's love. In the psalms Adam and Jenny found a script for moving from their worst fears to a powerful affirmation of trust. From the resentful, 'Hear my voice, O God, in my complaint' to the joyful, 'Hope in God; for I shall again praise him.'[110]

When lament psalms are used, what we may not be able to voice anywhere else may be shouted out in worship, even if they are words addressed to God whom it seems has abandoned us.

> My God, my God, why have you forsaken me?
>   Why are you so far from helping me, from the words of
>   my groaning?
>
> O my God, I cry by day, but you do not answer;
>   and by night, but find no rest.
>
> (Psalm 22:1-2)

Lament strips away religious politeness and tells it how it is. It tells God how it is. Lament psalms are also referred to as psalms of complaint: 'having it out with God,' complaining against God: 'Why

---

[110] Lischer, *Stations of the Heart*, 120–121.

The Grief Walk

have you walked out on me?' 'Why did this happen to us?' They dare to question the divine: 'Where are you?' 'When are you going to act?' 'Where's the justice?' C. S. Lewis' *A Grief Observed* is in the tradition of biblical lament. Lewis is trying to make sense of his grief.

> Meanwhile, where is God? This is one of the most disquieting symptoms. When you are happy, so happy that you have no sense of needing Him, so happy that you are tempted to feel His claims upon you as an interruption, if you remember yourself and turn to Him with gratitude and praise, you will be – or so it feels – welcomed with open arms. But go to Him when your need is desperate, when all other help is vain, and what do you find? A door slammed in your face, and a sound of bolting and double bolting on the inside. After that, silence. You may as well turn away. The longer you wait, the more emphatic the silence will become. There are no lights in the windows. It might be an empty house. Was it ever inhabited? It seemed so once. And that seeming was as strong as this. What can this mean? Why is He so present a commander in our time of prosperity and so very absent a help in time of trouble?[111]

Psalms of lament articulate these questions. They give words to our anger, fear, and bewilderment. They help us express our grief.

A man whose wife had recently died came to the church to share Morning Prayer with me. The psalm set down for the day contained these verses: 'Yet you have crushed us in a place of sorrows and covered us with the shadow of death... Why do you hide your face and forget our oppression and misery?' (Psalm 44:20, 25, *ANZPB*) Afterwards he remarked, 'Praying those lines helped me for the first time to tell God how I really felt.'

These psalms validate our experience of grief, and because specific circumstances aren't identified they can be applied to various experiences. They tell us that others have walked this road; others have shared our questions, our anger and hurt, our disorientation and confusion. The woman wondering if she will ever find employment

---

111 Lewis, *A Grief Observed*, 9.

again, the man facing another long night alone, the young person afraid of being rejected by mates, may find that the psalmist knows how it is; knows how it is to feel abandoned by God as well as friends.

While these psalms give expression to how I may feel, they have also taught me to listen more carefully to others, and to listen without judgement. A natural response is to try 'to fix' a situation, but grief isn't something to be 'solved.' I can't bring back the person who has died. I can't produce a baby for the couple grieving their childlessness. I can't erase the pain. What I can do is listen and be with the person grieving. Praying the lament psalms can help attune our ears to the grieving person as they give words to their pain.

Faith Incorporating Grief

Biblical lament can be cathartic, but it's far more than 'letting it all hang out.' Wrestling with the questions that permeate our lives, lamentation works to reconcile the tough stuff with the hope of our faith. Unlike David's dirge, biblical lament is God-focused, bringing together the divine and the human. Lament isn't the final destination but a journey towards God. Admittedly, it's a winding and tortuous road; nonetheless it's a journey towards something new.

> The spine of lament is hope, not the vacuous optimism that 'things will get better,' which in the short run is usually a lie, but the deep and irrepressible conviction, in the teeth of present evidence, that God has not severed the umbilical cord that has always bound us to the Lord.[112]

Lament never suppresses grief but walks a journey that encompasses it, integrating it into our relationship with God. Nicholas Wolterstorff observes:

> Some Christians find their loss so religiously disturbing that they give up on God and treasure their grief. Others seem to think that faith requires them to stifle their grief. What we see in the psalmist is a third way. Rather than grief without

---

112 Clifton Black, 'The Persistence of the Wounds' in *Lament: Reclaiming Practices in Pulpit, Pew, and Public Square,* ed. Sally Brown and Patrick D. Miller (Louisville: Westminster John Knox, 2005), 54.

> faith or faith without grief, we see faith incorporating grief. The psalmist's lament gives voice both to his grief and to the faith that incorporates his grief… I may eventually discover that a faith that incorporates grief is stronger and richer than a faith that sings only praise songs.'[113]

This isn't an easy process. Psalm 22, which is perhaps the best-known lament psalm as it opens with the words of abandonment that Jesus uttered on the cross (Mark 15:34, Matthew 27:46), assures us that that there is no shame in hurling our questions at God.

> My God, my God, why have you forsaken me?
>> Why are you so far from helping me, from the words of my groaning?
>
> O my God, I cry by day, but you do not answer;
>> and by night, but find no rest. (22:1–2)

This psalm reveals raw emotion:

> I am poured out like water,
>> and all my bones are out of joint;
>
> my heart is like wax;
>> it is melted within my breast;
>
> my mouth is dried up like a potsherd,
>> and my tongue sticks to my jaws;
>> you lay me in the dust of death. (22:14–15)

Yet there's the suggestion that, whatever the psalmist's present feelings, God has not deserted him. There's more to life with God, more to the life of God's people than this present experience of abandonment.

> In you our ancestors trusted;
>> they trusted, and you delivered them.
>
> To you they cried, and were saved;
>> in you they trusted, and were not put to shame. (22:4-5)

---

[113] Nicholas Wolterstorff, 'The Art of Lament', July 27, 2012. Accessed from https://www.thebanner.org/features/2012/07/the-art-of-lament

Words for our Grief – A Gift from the Psalms

The psalm reflects the circuitous course that grief can take. One moment we trust God, the next we want to blame God.

> My God, my God, why have you forsaken me? (22:1a)

> Yet you are holy,
> > enthroned on the praises of Israel. (22:3)

> But I am a worm, and not human… (22:6a)

> Yet it was you who took me from the womb;
> > you kept me safe on my mother's breast. (22:9)

> For dogs are all around me;
> > a company of evildoers encircles me. (22:16)

> But you, O Lord, do not be far away!
> O my help, come quickly to my aid! (22:19)

A similar pattern emerges in Psalm 42. In his distress the psalmist longs for God.

> My soul thirsts for God,
> > for the living God. (42:2)

Lament and trust are held together in tension. The psalmist's faith is bruised, even battered. Grief is his daily diet.

> My tears have been my food day and night,
> > while people say to me continually,
> > 'Where is your God?' (42:3)

Then the psalmist remembers how it was.

> how I went with the throng,
> > and led them in procession to the house of God,
>
> with glad shouts and songs of thanksgiving… (42:4)

But now it's different. Yet, in his distress, the psalmist finds that trust in God hasn't totally gone.

> Why are you cast down, O my soul,
> > and why are you disquieted within me?

> Hope in God; for I shall again praise him,
> my help and my God. (42:5–6)

Then grief again overwhelms him. Has God deserted him?

> I say to God, my rock,
> 'Why have you forgotten me?
>
> Why must I walk about mournfully
> because the enemy oppresses me?'
>
> As with a deadly wound in my body,
> my adversaries taunt me,
>
> while they say to me continually,
> 'Where is your God?' (42:9–10)

Finally, the voice of hope re-emerges.

> Why are you cast down, O my soul,
> and why are you disquieted within me?
>
> Hope in God; for I shall again praise him,
> my help and my God. (42:11)

This is how it often is with us. Grief doesn't follow a straight line. Doubt and trust, anger and harmony, lament and praise, all go hand in hand. Hope and trust finally emerge after a journey that takes many twists and turns. In this, these psalms are far more realistic than models of grief that describe a neat, linear course.

The strident tones of the lament psalms keep us from pretending all is well when it's not. By challenging our denial, they enable us to face the reality of our loss. Only when we are prepared to face head-on our individual and communal grief and acknowledge the accompanying disorientation can we begin to journey toward a new place.

We know that repressed grief can lead to mental and physical illness. In terms of our faith, unacknowledged grief leaves us feeling alone in our anguish, separated from others in our faith community, and separated from God. When we give lament a place in our communal life it can begin a process of healing. It helps those who are grieving to move towards wholeness, knowing that their distress and powerlessness has been heard and recognised. This isn't a magical remedy. Anguish and pain still lie within those who cry out, but the pain has been given a voice, one directed towards God, and that in itself is an act of faith. Questions don't move us away from God, but towards God. That's the nature and promise of lament.

Grief can help us encounter God in new and profound ways. It can be an instrument of healing and transformation, but that can only happen when we acknowledge the pain as it is. This is a foreign notion in our culture. We are encouraged to pop pills to deal with pain, but painkillers only mask the symptoms. They don't deal with the source. We have deluded ourselves into thinking that masking symptoms is tantamount to dealing with what caused the pain. So it is with grief. The lament psalms are a way of learning to face and speak about the cause. They take us on a journey that helps us to access our pain, and it's only by accessing it that we can we deal honestly with its cause. It's about becoming aware of and accepting our loss and grief; knowing that it truly matters.

My One Companion is Darkness

Psalm 88 is the darkest of all the psalms. Walter Brueggemann describes it as 'an embarrassment to conventional faith.'

> For my soul is full of troubles,
>   and my life draws near to Sheol.
>
> I am counted among those who go down to the Pit;
>   I am like those who have no help,
>
> like those forsaken among the dead,
>   like the slain that lie in the grave,
>
> like those whom you remember no more,
>   for they are cut off from your hand.
>
> You have put me in the depths of the Pit,
>   in the regions dark and deep.

> Your wrath lies heavy upon me,
>   and you overwhelm me with all your waves.
>
> You have caused my companions to shun me;
>   you have made me a thing of horror to them.
>
> I am shut in so that I cannot escape;
>   my eye grows dim through sorrow.
>
> Every day I call on you, O Lord;
>   I spread out my hands to you. (88:3–9)

For those who get tired of faking it when times are tough, this is your psalm. It's dark and it's dismal. God isn't let off the hook. The psalmist has been deserted and says so. Unlike other psalms of lament, this one doesn't come to a point of trust in God. There's no resolution. The final words are words of darkness.

> You have caused friend and neighbour to shun me;
>   my companions are in darkness. (88:18)

Or, as other translations have it, '… all that I know is dark' (*NJB*) … 'Darkness is my closest friend.' (*NLT*).

Why is this psalm in Scripture? Because the psalms reflect life as it actually is; not just the good parts but also the darkest. Psalm 88 mirrors our experiences at the darkest of times when we feel abandoned, especially by God. Yet, it's still speech, and speech directed at God, and that in itself speaks of faith. Walter Brueggemann, a pre-eminent biblical scholar, goes further, saying they are bold acts of faith.

> The use of these 'psalms of darkness' may be judged by the world to be *acts of unfaith and failure*, but for the trusting community, their use is *an act of bold faith*, albeit a transformed faith. It is an act of bold faith on the one hand, because it insists that the world must be experienced as it really is and not in some pretended way. On the other hand, it is bold because it insists that all such experiences of disorder are a proper subject for discourse with God. There is nothing out of bounds, nothing precluded or inappropriate. Everything properly belongs in the conversation of the heart. To withhold parts of life from that conversation is in fact

> to withhold part of life from the sovereignty of God... But such faith is indeed a *transformed* faith... The community that uses these psalms of disorientation... (expresses faith in a God) who is present in, participating in, and attentive to the darkness, weakness, and displacement of life. The god assumed by and addressed in these psalms is a God 'of sorrows, and acquainted with grief.'[114]

This, the darkest of all psalms, affirms that persistent prayer, even when there is no sign of a response from a seemingly absent god, is an act of faith – bold faith.

Darkness, in whatever way we experience it, is common to our experience of grief and we may wonder how it can have a place in the Christian journey. After all, as John begins his Gospel, he declares, 'The light that shines in the darkness, and the darkness did not overcome it' (1:5). Some of the religious words that are spoken to those who are grieving are an attempt to deny the darkness because we are afraid of it: 'It's all part of God's plan.' 'Your faith is strong enough to overcome this.' We need to recognise darkness for what it is: darkness. Don't pretend it's something else. Then, instead of avoiding it, we can learn to live with it in a creative and courageous way.

Jennifer's Dad's vehicle was involved in a motor crash. The impact caused his car to explode and the flames consumed his body. Jennifer writes:

> It hurts when someone says that darkness is not so dark, because it attempts to diminish the pain of grief and in so doing strikes at the love from which that grief is born. From inside, I knew what was darkness, and not only did I not want it to be diminished, my stripped soul had no desire for that parade of imitations that I know were not real in comparison to the flickers of a Light that I was beginning to see. From inside, I have come to believe that the greatest tragedy is that when we shield ourselves from that darkness,

---

114 Walter Brueggemann, *The Message of the Psalms: A Theological Commentary* (Minneapolis: Augsburg Press, 1984), 52.

we also shade ourselves from the Light… 'What has come into being in him was life, and the life was the light of all people. The light shines in the darkness, and the darkness did not overcome it' (John 1:3–5). Believing in the Light does not mean that the darkness ceases to exist. No, the Light comes into the darkness and is not overcome by it.

Real hope can only be conceived in the darkness, when we leave a place for it.[115]

Challenging a Cover-up

By and large the church prefers not to know the darkness. We prefer to sing joyful songs of praise and triumph. We might claim that these are an affirmation of God's victory over death and loss. Perhaps, but more often than not, they reflect the fact that we have succumbed to the prevailing cultural denial of loss and grief, death and bereavement. We are satisfied to offer spiritual painkillers that mask the symptoms but don't embrace the cause. To cite Walter Brueggemann again:

> Such a denial and cover-up, which I take it to be, is an odd inclination for passionate Bible users, given the large number of psalms that are songs of lament, protest, and complaint about the incoherence that is experienced in the world. At least it is clear that a church that goes on singing 'happy songs' in the face of raw reality is doing something very different from what the Bible itself does.
>
> I think that serious religious use of the lament psalms has been minimal because we have believed that faith does not mean to acknowledge and embrace negativity. We have thought that acknowledgement of negativity was somehow an act of unfaith, as though the very speech about it conceded too much about God's 'loss of control.'[116]

---

[115] Jennifer Replogle, 'New life I never wanted' in *Inside Grief*, Stephen Oliver (ed.) (London: SPCK, 2013), 35–36.
[116] Brueggemann, *The Message of the Psalms*, 51-52.

Words for our Grief – A Gift from the Psalms

The lament psalms contest the illusion that all is well. They break through our pretence that life is well ordered when it's not. The denial may be of a broken relationship or a lost job, a medical diagnosis, or that death is simply a matter of 'passing away.' The abrasive words of these psalms penetrate the deception and say, 'No, this is how it is!' No wonder we avoid these psalms. They lead us into the harsh reality of human existence. They challenge the illusion that we can manage and control everything.

> In our modern experience… it is believed that enough power and knowledge can tame the terror and eliminate the darkness… But our honest experience, both personal and public, attests to the resilience of the darkness, in spite of us. The remarkable thing about Israel is that it did not banish or deny the darkness from its religious enterprise. It embraces the darkness as the very stuff of new life. Indeed, Israel seems to know that new life comes nowhere else.[117]

In my tradition the psalms are included in most public services, but we have succumbed to this cover up. In 'Psalms for Worship' in *A New Zealand Prayer Book – He Karakia Mihinare o Aotearoa*, verses have been omitted, implying they are deemed inappropriate for Christian worship. Some examples:

> Repay them according to their work,
>   and according to the evil of their deeds;
>
> repay them according to the work of their hands;
>   render them their due reward. (Psalm 28:4)

Or

> Let their eyes be darkened so that they cannot see,
>   and make their loins tremble continually.
>
> Pour out your indignation upon them,
>   and let your burning anger overtake them.
>
> May their camp be a desolation;
>   let no one live in their tents.

---

[117] Brueggemann, *The Message of the Psalms*, 53.

> For they persecute those whom you have struck down,
> > and those whom you have wounded, they attack still more
>
> Add guilt to their guilt;
> > may they have no acquittal from you.
>
> Let them be blotted out of the book of the living;
> > let them not be enrolled among the righteous.
> > (Psalm 69: 23–28)

These words may not sound 'very Christian and loving.' But whatever arguments are put up for their exclusion, their omission reveals a lack of appreciation for what lament is and the nature of grief. Such raw words are integral to how we may feel in the midst of deep suffering. I think of a parent who has just learned that a close relation has been sexually abusing their child, and a woman whose husband has been killed by a drunk driver. These verses give words to how they may well feel. They articulate what is in the heart, even though the parent and the woman dare not voice them for fear of being told 'You shouldn't feel that. You must forgive.' Everything that we experience and feel has a rightful place in our prayer. To withhold parts of our life from our prayer is to withhold part of ourselves from God.

I challenge the church in all its traditions to restore lament to the life of our faith communities. When did your faith community last make space within its worship for the cry of anguish? I wonder how people might respond if you advertised: 'You are invited to a good lament – this Sunday at 10.00am.'

Many of our funeral services rush to talk about the light and life that the darkness of death cannot overcome, but what place is given to the darkness of grief? Celebrate the life of the deceased, by all means, but also face up to the death of this irreplaceable and precious life and weep all the tears you have in you to weep. A death of one we love is like the death of part of us.

Grief, with its accompanying dark and painful forces, has been banished. Little wonder, lament is hardly good news, but this banishment is to our detriment. As psychology teaches us, there is a high price to be paid if we ignore our grief. When we make no room for lament, we hide away the painful realities of human experience and marginalise those who are suffering. But if we retrieve lament and give it its rightful place, we may renew our capacity for compassion, for we shall be giving a voice to those who are grieving and suffering.

Lament fosters solidarity with those suffering among us. Some days I read a psalm of lament when all I want to do is celebrate. But as I pray the words of pain and sorrow, of rejection and frustration, grief and anger, I offer them for those for whom these experiences are all too real. A devastating effect of grief is the isolation that it causes. The sufferer often feels alone, disconnected and abandoned. To share communal lament enables authentic community. It builds a faith community in which those who are suffering realise they aren't alone, that it's acceptable to hurt and be vulnerable. It may give them permission (as well as the language) to say what otherwise is hushed up. In a community where this happens those who are grieving may meet those who 'weep with those who weep'. The words of lament bring us into the company of those who suffer; they also take us by the hand and lead us into the presence of God who shares our suffering. This encounter may well be shrouded in darkness, none the less, it's a real encounter that reveals God walking with us in the darkest places.

Ben Johnson-Frow is a parish priest and singer-songwriter who composed this lament.

> Broken and alone
> Crushed and overwhelmed
> Fearful far from home
> Where are you Lord?
>
> In the past, you have comforted me
> Planted by a stream
> But now I'm far too weary
> Tired, but cannot sleep
>
> Night times are the worst
> When you feel like no one lives
> Night times are the worst
> When you feel like something must give

The Grief Walk

> Though my eyes begin to fade
> Still my mouth is filled with praise
> Through the cracks a light appears
> Saviour draw near
>
> I'm not broken… I am blessed.[118]

Ben may reflect the experience of many of us when he speaks of the night times being the worst. In grief this can be the hardest of times. Reflecting on his own writing, and the experience of the psalmists, Ben comments:

> You can imagine the writer expressing how he's feeling and someone saying one of those useless pieces of advice that people sometimes give like 'Oh, you should just try and get more sleep then, have an early night' – and the response from the psalmist is 'actually – Night times are the worst…' It's the time when grief presses down and no one else can be there for you. It leads to that desperate feeling of just hanging on till the dawn.

---

118 Benjamin P. Johnson-Frow, 2019.

10 – Walking with Job – A Story of Losing and Grieving[119]

Few biblical stories resonate more loudly with those who sit among the ashes of grief than that of Job. The book that carries his name was written by an unknown author who uses an ancient tale as the setting to probe the depths of faith in the midst of suffering. It poses the tough questions that dog many of us when we face suffering 'for no reason' (2:3). The book doesn't supply neat answers to our questions, but it reminds us that we are not alone in asking them.

Job incorporates many of the issues and questions that I voice throughout this book. As the Psalms can become our words, so Job's story can be our story. Because most of Job is in poetic form, and poetry has a way of reaching the heart that prose doesn't, we have a vehicle that enables us to be with our own stories of loss and suffering, to ask our questions and to wrestle with God.

Job's losses are familiar to many: the loss of possessions and livelihood, the sudden loss of health through chronic illness. The death of his servants, then his children, triggers the memory of deaths we have known of colleagues, friends, and family members. As one loss comes to mind, others may well follow, and as they do, honour your grief and give it voice, joining with Job who yearned to be heard.

The Scene is Set – Job 1:1 – 2:10

We are introduced to a man who is totally devoted to God. Not only is Job wise and virtuous, he has everything a person of his time could hope for: a large family, material wealth, good health, and the respect of all who knew him, 'so this man was the greatest of all the people of the east.' With the scene set, the story turns to the heavenly realms where a conversation is taking place between God and a figure called Satan (the Hebrew *ha-satan*, meaning *the accuser* or *adversary*, not

---

119 This chapter draws substantially on a paper that Deborah Broome and I co-authored: 'More than a multitude of words? Pastoral Care for Job and his family' (Wellington Institute of Theology – Anglican Diocese of Wellington, October 2012).

the evil character of later Christian thought). God is rather proud of Job: 'There is no one like him on the earth, a blameless and upright man who fears God and turns away from evil.' Satan isn't impressed. After all, look how much Job has been blessed with good fortune. Clearly, he's God's favourite. So, Satan puts a proposition to God. Take away everything Job has and see how faithful Job is then. He will then 'curse you to your face.' God accepts the challenge.

Job suffers a string of tragedies and loses almost everything. First, his livestock are stolen or destroyed, most of his servants are killed, and then a tornado strikes the house where his ten children are staying, killing them all. Job's response is impeccable, 'Naked I came from my mother's womb, and naked shall I return there; the Lord gave, and the Lord has taken away; blessed be the name of the Lord.' Job responds to his suffering with acceptance and trust in God. Having lost so much, Job sits among the ashes. In the face of these multiple losses, and even though the weight of grief is almost too much to bear, Job retains his trust in God. This is too much for his wife: 'Do you still persist in your integrity? Curse God, and die.' But Job remains faithful to God, and it would seem God has won the challenge.

Job's Friends – Job 2:11–13

Integral to the story are three friends: Eliphaz, Bildad, and Zophar. It's from them that the term 'Job's comforter' comes: a person who tries to console or help someone and not only fails but ends up making the other feel worse. The friends get bad press, and yes, Job will later call them 'miserable comforters,' but they did get some things right.

What the Friends got Right

Faced with his losses, Job 'tore his robe, shaved his head, and fell on the ground' and then went and sat among the ashes. He is following traditional Jewish mourning rituals, as do his three friends. On hearing of Job's troubles, they went to 'console and comfort him,' and when they arrived, they didn't recognise him, and no wonder. Sitting alone among the ashes, his body festering with sores, racked with pain, emaciated and disfigured – Job isn't pleasant company. While our symptoms may differ, how many of us in grief present as pleasant company? Those close to Job have deserted him, but not these three. They are prepared to travel some distance to be with him. They are caring and have good intentions and while they get many things wrong, let it be remembered, they turn up and are prepared to sit with him 'for seven days and seven nights.'

These three are not deterred, even, when what they find is so shocking 'they did not recognise him;' such was the impact of Job's suffering. He who 'was the greatest of all the people of the east' had acquired a 'greatness' of a very different kind: 'his suffering was very great.' It's so easy to walk by when what we see isn't pleasant. Caring for others can sound noble, but what if those we are called to care for are no longer dignified, respectable, or gracious? Do we stay, let alone for seven days and seven nights?

The friends know how to act, and they know what Job needs. They are able to draw on customs that help people deal with grief. It's a process that's not limited to words but involves actions and recognises that we need time to be with our grief, time to find new meaning, and time to reintegrate into society. Compare this to how people find themselves today. Having dispensed with religion and a traditional sense of community, many in our culture have lost the reference points that provide stability in times of acute instability. In the midst of the chaos that accompanies grief people are at sea. When they grieve deeply, they are on a journey into the unknown, into a wilderness where there are few if any signposts to guide them.

Sitting Shiva

What's described here is traditional Jewish mourning, and if any tradition knows how to mourn, it's Judaism. Mourning is never easy, but it's best done within a communal context. Lauren Winner, who converted from Orthodox Judaism to Christianity, observes that while Christianity has a hopeful and true vocabulary for death-and-resurrection, it's Judaism that has the grammar for mourning. 'Judaism understands mourning as a discipline, one in which the mourner is not only allowed, but expected, to be engaged.'[120] Judaism

---

120 Lauren F. Winner, *Mudhouse Sabbath: An Invitation to a Life of Spiritual Discipline* (Brewster, Massachusetts: Paraclete Press, 2010), 28.

The Grief Walk

knows that grief takes time and the bereaved need others; that it's a good thing for others to witness our grief stricken sighs, to share our memories and pray our prayers with us. 'They met together to go and console and comfort him.' Within our faith communities the ministry of comfort and consolation ought not be reserved to a few but be the calling of the entire community.

Following a death, Judaism sets a year aside for mourning, and the seven days following the burial are *shiva,* during which the immediate family will remain at home to be visited and comforted. They will 'sit *shiva,*' as Job's friends did for seven days. The men remain unshaven and the women wear no make-up, not leaving the house except on *Shabbat* (the weekly day of rest and renewal). Relatives, friends and neighbours bring food to the bereaved household. During *shiva* the house of mourning will become crowded as people meet, talk, and eat.

The friends respond to Job, not with words, but with gestures of mourning. They share in Job's suffering through ritual. 'They raised their voices and wept aloud; they tore their robes and threw dust in the air upon their heads. They sat with him on the ground for seven days and seven nights...' This is ritual of the deepest kind. They are symbolically sharing in Job's affliction. Interestingly, the Hebrew behind the words *console* and *comfort* refers to a bodily movement, as when we shake our head in sympathy with another's plight. The movement enacts the sympathy and identifies in a bodily way our expression of compassion.

When we witness deep distress and suffering in others, we are often lost for words. All we can do is shake our heads. There are no words to be said – at least, none that will suffice. Reflecting on his father's funeral, Sam Hunt wrote:

> Friends, men met on the road,
> stood round in that dumb way
> men stand when lost for words.
> There was nothing to say.[121]

---

121 Sam Hunt, 'My Father Today' in *Moonlight: New Zealand Poems on Death and Dying,* Andrew Johnston (ed.) (Auckland; Godwit, 2008), 86–87.

Job's friends enact the rituals of loss and grief and they get one other thing very right. 'They sat with him… and no one spoke a word to him…' The consolation and comfort they offer is the gift of shared silence. There's no magic power that banishes grief. It's no comfort to be told that fervent prayer or stronger faith will vanquish the pain of loss. But there's comfort in the quiet, faithful, compassionate presence of those who sit *shiva* with us. Comfort is, first of all, presence: being there, listening, and sitting beside us on our mourning bench. We tend to fill the silence with words, but at this point silence is what Job needed. It allowed him to enter into his brokenness and loss.

Earlier, Job uttered the memorable words: 'Naked I came from my mother's womb, and naked shall I return there; the Lord gave, and the Lord has taken away; blessed be the name of the Lord.' They are eloquent words, but they didn't meet the reality of his experience. Suffering should silence praise that's too glib and disconnected from reality. Job's grief was so big that silence was the only response that could accommodate the enormity of his pain and suffering. As I spend more and more time with people who are grieving, I find that I have fewer and fewer words. Suffering of any ilk can be overwhelming. These experiences often strike me as too profound, too significant for ordinary words. Sometimes all I can offer are simple actions and rituals that transcend words. I'm learning to be honest about that and I allow a hand held in silence or a gentle hug to express what I have no words for.

Silence isn't the end of faith; it may be its true beginning. In the silence Job has begun to enter his pain and embark on his search for new meaning. His friends have helped him in this, but now they get many things wrong and become 'miserable comforters.'

What the Friends got Wrong

Eliphaz, Bildad and Zophar are helpful companions until Job can no longer keep silent. He must now speak, and he pours out his anguish and despair (chapter 3). The three friends don't know how to listen. They spend the time while Job is talking self-listening, working out what they are going to say in reply. They hear his words, but they are not listening to what Job is saying and, crucially, they are not

The Grief Walk

listening to the emotions behind his outbursts. When they open their mouths, they say the wrong things.

Silence recognises that in the presence of deep grief words can be acutely inadequate. This doesn't mean we should say nothing for fear of saying the wrong thing. Saying something can be helpful, especially if it shows the person they aren't alone in their pain. A tentative beginning such as Eliphaz makes: 'If one ventures a word with you, will you be offended?' (4:2), coupled with an honest admission that we don't know what to say, can be of comfort. Some approaches though, are clearly wrong. Blaming Job's children for their own death is out-and-out crass. 'Your children must have sinned against [God], so their punishment was well deserved' (8:4 *NLT*). We see this lack of empathy elsewhere, for example, when Zophar tells Job that God has been soft on him: 'God is doubtless punishing you far less than you deserve!' (11:6 *NLT*)

As time goes on, they all become argumentative. This includes Job, and in this he epitomises what can happen when we are dealing with tough personal stuff: we express strong emotions and it's natural to vent. Wise friends simply listen and acknowledge the need of the grieving person to say whatever they need to say without having to face contradiction or correction. They listen and affirm the validity of the person's pain and the questions they express.

The friends can't resist explaining Job's losses (see chapters 4, 8, 11, 15, 18, 20, 22, and 25). There must be a good reason for his misfortune. They are all locked into a worldview that's based on reward and punishment. The three assume they know why such dreadful things have occurred to Job and his family. It's because Job has sinned, and he needs to repent. In other words, bad things happen to bad people, just as good things happen to good people. Even if suffering can be explained and justified by pointing to the sufferer's own wrongdoing ('He deserved this' … 'She had it coming to her'), to say so adds insult to injury, and makes the suffering worse. Blaming the victim doesn't help. Saying, 'Well of course you've got lung cancer, that's what happens if you smoke 30 a day for 40 years' isn't only negative but totally unnecessary: is this not what sufferers so often are saying to themselves anyway? The other explanation that's often given, and which is in line with the approach taken by the three friends, is: God is trying to teach you a valuable lesson.

Friends often mean well, though their responses are inappropriate because they don't understand the nature of loss and grief. At other times friends' behaviour isn't so benign. As we walk through our grief, we may well lose some friends. A pastor who specialises in journeying with people who are grieving reflects on this hard reality.

> They may be engaging in a wilful, if unconscious, attempt to build a defence against their own fear of loss. By finding a reason to blame us for our loss, or to at least explain it as something specific to us, they may be trying to reassure themselves that they won't have to face a similar loss. And sometimes our friends will just 'disappear,' literally or figuratively. Perhaps they fear, even unconsciously, that our misfortune may rub off on them.[122]

This was Job's experience.

> My relatives stay far away,
>   and my friends have turned against me.
>
> My family is gone,
>   and my close friends have forgotten me.
>
> My servants and maids consider me a stranger.
>   I am like a foreigner to them.
>
> My close friends detest me.
>   Those I loved have turned against me.
>   (19:13–15,19 *NLT*)

Friends who know how to come close and sit with a person who is grieving, to share the silence and hear the questions, to share tears and recognise the pain are a treasured gift. Their presence, the gift of caring companionship, helps sustain the grieving person. Sadly, it's not uncommon for the pain of loss to be compounded by a secondary loss: the sudden or gradual fading of friendships when friends

---

[122] John T. Schwiebert, 'The Book of Job: A Three Thousand-Year-Old Story of Grief – Pt. Two: Miserable Comforters'. Accessed from https://griefwatch.com/the-book-of-job-part-two/?SID=60be9bb544d610648ad1774adcb8c2c0

cannot cope with the pain of another person's grief. Or when friends add to the pain by responding in unhelpful and inappropriate ways. The good news is that, in supportive groups and in communities where our pain and grief is accepted without judgement, we find new friends who will journey with us in our grief because they have already walked the path of grief and know how to be with us without trying to judge us or fix us. They allow us to be with our grief.

Reading through the book of Job we hear the four of them argue backwards and forwards. The three friends are unable to put aside their theological assumptions. Job's losses must be a punishment for, or at least a consequence of, some unconfessed sin. When we are presented with suffering, logical theories (including deeply held religious ones) are inadequate. Job's multiple losses have left him emotionally battered, feeling betrayed by his community and by God. Like many pastors, I've learned that a Theology 101 tutorial isn't the answer to a broken heart.

Why do the three friends, like many people today, behave like this? I see two possible reasons. First, they felt threatened by what had happened to Job. If such a well-regarded man could lose everything in this way, could the same tragedy one day befall them? If Job can admit that this was just punishment for some sin, then they can feel secure that as long as they behave themselves, they will be all right. So, they hold tightly to their beliefs because it gives them a sense of control over their own destiny. Second, they feel they have to come up with an answer. They can't cope with Job's suffering; they can't sit with his emotional pain or let his questions simply hang in the air. But to journey with others requires that we allow the tough questions to be voiced without rushing in with an answer. I often wish I could wave a magic pastoral wand and transform the dust and cinders into a happy ending, but I can't, any more than you can.

Job's Wife

Another character that emerges, almost as a footnote, is Job's wife. Job isn't the only suffering individual here. His wife has also lost all her worldly goods, her social position, and the respect of those who looked up to her as the wife of a great man. And, even worse, she too has lost all her children. In a society where a woman's worth was as a mother, especially of sons, she is now worthless, as well as grieving. Yet no one comforts her. If Eliphaz, Bildad, and Zophar meet together to go and console and comfort Job, where were their wives? Where were the women of the community who could gather around Job's wife? She represents the disenfranchised grievers, those who have lost much, but whose loss and grief isn't acknowledged.

What Job Needed – Giving Voice to his Grief

Initially, shared silence may be the only response we can give to intense grief. When the time comes for words to be spoken, what is needed are not arguments but the opportunity to voice our pain.

> As long as one stays in silence, one searches alone. It is when silence gives way to speech that sufferers begin a journey that advances faith to a new level. Once spoken, pain can be named for what it is. It can be addressed, engaged, questioned, refuted, attacked. The very act of speaking in the midst of pain and suffering is an act of faith. It signals a fierce resolve to believe that someone will listen, someone will care, someone will come.[123]

The time it takes to move from silence to voice varies from person to person. Now it's Job's time. His world has collapsed. Life is meaningless. God doesn't care. Job breaks the silence and cries out, damning the day he was born.

> Let the day perish on which I was born,
>   and the night that said,
>   'A man-child is conceived.'
>
> Let that day be darkness!
>   May God above not seek it,
>   or light shine on it...'
>
> 'Why did I not die at birth,
>   come forth from the womb and expire? ...

---

[123] Samuel E. Balentine, *Job – Smyth and Helwys Bible Commentary* (Macon, Georgia: Smyth & Helwys Publishing, 2006), 96.

> Or why was I not buried like a stillborn child,
>   like an infant that never sees the light? ...
>
> For my sighing comes like my bread,
>   and my groanings are poured out like water.
>   (3:3–4, 11, 16, 24)

Anger and the Need to Blame

Job's words match his anguish and give voice to his pain. The heart must speak honestly. Such words may not change anything, but they show that Job isn't prepared to be a victim and they express a hope that somehow things should be different. When we are struggling to find meaning, we can't – we mustn't – tone it down:

> Therefore I will not restrain my mouth;
> I will speak in the anguish of my spirit;
> I will complain in the bitterness of my soul. (7:11)

Job's response is echoed in Shakespeare's *Macbeth*. Ross delivers to Macduff the tragic news of the murder of his wife and children. He describes them as 'words that would be howl'd out in the desert air.' Deep distress seeks words and, overhearing this news, Malcolm urges him,

> Give sorrow words: the grief that does not speak
> Whispers the o'er-fraught heart and bids it break. (IV, iii)

These lines encourage the expression of grief, but what about the words that follow? Macduff's emotions are complex. He's torn between guilt and anger. He wants to act and seek revenge, and Malcolm endorses this decision, saying,

> ... let grief
> Convert to anger; blunt not the heart; enrage it.

Not always, but often, anger is integral to grief. We may, like Macduff, search for someone or something to blame. We look for a reason for our loss. Our anger may be irrational and unreasonable, yet it seems there's a need to find a cause on which to hang responsibility for our loss. Martha Nussbaum suggests that it may be 'better that there should be someone to blame than that the universe should be a place of accident in which one's loved ones are helpless. Blame is a valuable antidote to helplessness.'[124]

The description of the universe as 'a place of accident' reflects Job's suffering 'for no reason.' We want an explanation. We need to lay the cause of loss down to someone or something, and when we can't, anger abounds: the anger of frustration and impotence. Many of us who have been raised in a Christian culture picked up the belief that anger is out of place in our faith, but Scripture doesn't support this. Anger abounds in the book of Job. We first meet it in chapter 3 when Job lets God have it with no holds barred. He speaks in the lament tradition: the unashamed words of disorientation, protest, complaint, anger, and despair.

Job's Questioning

Job's lament comes in the form of a series of heart-wrenching questions. 'Why did I not die at birth?' 'Why is light given to one who cannot see the way?' Under the weight of suffering everything comes under review. It throws up questions about our deepest beliefs. In Gail Godwin's novel *Evensong*, a young woman who is training to be a priest is ministering in a hospital. Disheartened by the suffering she feels powerless to alleviate, she asks an older priest, 'Where is God in all this?' He replies:

> Your question may be the only one that matters. Despite the convoluted guesswork by theologians ever since Job's friends hunched beside him on the dung heap, 'Where is God in this?' (just the question alone, I mean) may be enough to keep us busy down here. Maybe the thing we're required to do is simply keep asking the question as Job did – asking it faithfully over and over – until God begins to reveal himself through the ways we are changed by the answering silence.[125]

I can't overstress the importance of giving people the freedom to question. Questions reverberate throughout the book of Job and of

---

124 M. Nussbaum, *Upheavals of Thought: The Intelligence of Emotions* (Cambridge: Cambridge University Press, 2001), 29. n. 19.
125 Gail Godwin, *Evensong*, (New York: Ballantine Books, 1999). Accessed from: https://www.gailgodwin.com/book-excerpt.php?isbn13=9780345434777

all questions 'Why' may be the most searching. How do we respond? With platitudes or neat theological answers? No! That's the mistake made by Job's friends. The person in pain needs the freedom to ask the question, knowing that it's been heard and accepted. Pam Heaney puts it well.

> 'Why' is not seeking a ready answer, nor is it wishing to be silenced. It is a passionate cry of anguish and is the start of a process that strives to gain some insight into how the world works and what life is about. It seeks meaning and purpose and is a cry from the deepest most primal part of our being that needs connection with something which is infinite and greater than the grief that overwhelms us.[126]

It's not a matter of agreeing or disagreeing with the questions posed or the statements made, still less criticising or correcting them. What is required is that we listen to them and take them seriously, without feeling threatened or outraged. We must learn to put aside our need to come up with answers, because sometimes there are no answers – at least, none that will suffice.

Job's grief left him in a state of spiritual and emotional chaos. He would express trust in God, blessing God's goodness, then, the next moment, curse God's injustice. He insists on his innocence and then he doubts. Perhaps the friends are right?

> Though I am innocent,
>   my own mouth would condemn me;
>   though I am blameless, he would prove me perverse.
>
> I am blameless; I do not know myself;
>   I loathe my life.
>
> It is all one; therefore I say,
>   he destroys both the blameless and the wicked. (9:20–22)

Job's doubt is intensified when he, as a bereaved parent, sees other parents with less integrity than he thriving and enjoying their children while he grieves.

---

126 Heaney, *Coming to Grief,* 43.

> Why do the wicked live on,
>   reach old age, and grow mighty in power? ...
>
> Their houses are safe from fear,
>   and no rod of God is upon them...
>
> They send out their little ones like a flock,
>   and their children dance around...
>
> They spend their days in prosperity,
>   and in peace they go down to Sheol. (21:7, 9, 11, 13)

Questions abound, and that's common in grief. We cry out: 'None of this makes sense!' ... 'Why me?' ... 'Where is God in all this?' These are the questions of lament.

> Today also my complaint is bitter;
>   his hand is heavy despite my groaning.
>
> O that I knew where I might find him,
>   that I might come even to his dwelling!...
>
> If I go forward, he is not there;
>   or backward, I cannot perceive him;
>
> on the left he hides, and I cannot behold him;
>   I turn to the right, but I cannot see him...
>
> If only I could vanish in darkness,
>   and thick darkness would cover my face! (23:2–3, 8–9, 17)

Job's comforters can't cope with this outpouring of raw emotion. As people have done down the ages, they trot out religious clichés, but Job will have none of this. He turns his anger and accusations towards God.

> I was at ease, and [God] broke me in two;
>   he seized me by the neck and dashed me to pieces;
>
> he set me up as his target;
>   his archers surround me.

> He slashes open my kidneys, and shows no mercy;
> > he pours out my gall on the ground.
>
> He bursts upon me again and again;
> > he rushes at me like a warrior.
>
> I have sewed sackcloth upon my skin,
> > and have laid my strength in the dust.
>
> My face is red with weeping,
> > and deep darkness is on my eyelids,
>
> though there is no violence in my hands,
> > and my prayer is pure. (16:12–17)

Faith Containing Tensions

Job reveals the tensions that exist in faith. We can praise and lament; affirm and question; accept and rage; trust and doubt. Doubt and anger are not opposites of faith, but elements of faith. Our willingness to articulate them is an expression of a faith that's prepared to face reality, believing that God accepts such radical dialogue. It also says that we are not prepared to be victims. It's the cry for meaning and hope.

There are times we must simply accept that the night is dark and admit our fears of the darkness of the world and of our own lives. Sometimes, whether we are Job's companions or Job himself, we need to sit through the silence, until the night heralds the dawn and the possibilities of a new day. We cannot rush these things, nor should we try. This is where Job's friends failed. The tensions and ambiguities Job voiced were too much for them. There was, however, someone who does understand, and that someone has been listening all along: God. Unlike anyone else in this book, God can cope with Job's anger and questioning, but God doesn't generally respond in the simple, straightforward way that we want. Often the response is silence, but then we must, like Job, be willing to hear God's questions. Suffering presents questions, and in the context of Job's story, they point to his readiness to go somewhere new and experience a spirituality never before imagined.

The Climax – Job 38–41

In these final chapters we hear God's response as God leads Job into a larger world where he might see what it means to be fully human, and what it means for God to be God. God has allowed Job to rant and rave and ask his questions. Now that Job feels that God has registered his complaint, he's ready to learn again the value of silence. Job answers the Lord:

> See, I am of small account; what shall I answer you?
>   I lay my hand on my mouth.
>
> I have spoken once, and I will not answer;
>   twice, but will proceed no further. (40:4–5)

This is a different kind of silence: the silence of one who feels heard and who is beginning to discover a transformed faith. God speaks again, and Job replies:

> I know that you can do all things,
>   and that no purpose of yours can be thwarted…
>
> Therefore I have uttered what I did not understand,
>   things too wonderful for me,
>   which I did not know…
>
> I had heard of you by the hearing of the ear,
>   but now my eye sees you;
>
> therefore I despise myself,
>   and repent in dust and ashes. (42:2, 3b–6)

What Job had *heard* was the traditional understanding of God; it was what his friends kept coming back to him with, and he found it totally unacceptable because it didn't fit with his experience. Now, at the climax of the book, he declares, 'now my eye *sees* you…' *Seeing* God is code for a personal, first-hand experience of God.

Through the path of multiple and traumatic loss Job has discovered something new and transformative. He has grasped a new vision of life, of himself, of God. Marcus Borg summarises where Job has come to.

The Grief Walk

> Job's experience of God gave him no new answers or explanations for the problem of suffering. But his experience convinced him that God was real in spite of the human inability to see fairness in the world. His experience of God changed him: 'Therefore I melt into nothingness, and repent in dust and ashes,' he said. As his old construction of the world (and himself) melted away, he 'repented' – that is, he changed.[127]

Job's grief isn't eliminated; it will always be a part of him. Life after a significant loss is never the same. As we question beliefs and values that we previously took for granted our worldview changes. How we see life changes, and our relationship with God also changes, perhaps, as it did for Job, radically. Job has flung his heart-wrenching questions at God, wrestling with God in anger and despair. Job doesn't receive answers to his questions about suffering. He doesn't fully understand why these things happened to him (and somehow, he accepts this), but he has begun to find a new trust in God, a recreated relationship with God. He now sees the world in such a way that he has an appetite for discovering a new life.

Our Faith may be Challenged and Changed

Our experience of grief may challenge and change what we believe and how we relate to God. But one thing I have learned: faith is brave enough to ask questions and to live with silence. Beth Allen Slevcove has it right when she says:

> This seems to be the pattern: We think we know who God is and who we are in relation to God, our understandings are shattered through some experience, God comes along and eventually gives us a new and greater understanding of God, and just when we think we've got it figured out, the cycle repeats.[128]

---

127 Marcus J. Borg, *Reading the Bible for the First Time: Taking the Bible Seriously but Not Literally* (New York: Harper Collins, 2002), 178. Borg suggests that 'I melt into nothingness' is a better translation than 'I despise myself,' and 'repent in dust and ashes' does not mean Job was guilty of great sins but that the experience changed him. n.56, 182.
128 Slevcove, *Broken Hallelujahs,* 64.

Nicholas Wolterstorff, reflecting on his son's death, tells of how a rabbi friend who participated in the funeral by reading from the Hebrew Scriptures, remarked afterward that he witnessed 'the endurance of faith.'

> He was right: my faith endured. But it would become a different kind of faith, a faith that incorporated Eric's death and my grief. And that would reveal to me a different kind of God, more mysterious. My relationship with my fellow human beings also changed: I felt an emotional affinity, often unspoken, with those whom I knew were also in grief.[129]

At the heart of Christian life is relationship with God, and as with our human relationships, this relationship is never static. It's subject to constant change and challenge which can lead to something new. This isn't to say a specific loss is necessary for growth. God doesn't give our loved one a terminal illness, or us an experience of suffering, that we might be a better person. That isn't a god I can believe in. Rather, the shattered expectations and hopes, the loss of a belief, the failures, the questions that we wrestle with, can be instruments of transformation.

---

129 Nicholas Wolterstorff, 'On grief, and not theologizing about it', 10 January 2019. Accessed from https://www.christiancentury.org/article/first-person/grief-and-not-theologizing-about-it?fbclid=IwAR1_uh-DasitGMqzjXvnCl-b31bUMQWPm5Hw8gC1UbEtn0ttr6quh4Fwbl4

11 – The Easter Walk

When life is tough, I want God to do something. I'm not always sure what, but some part of me looks to God to intervene. But I've discovered that before anything can happen, I have to face and experience the pain. I need to engage with it – I need to embrace it. That's hard because it involves waiting… waiting in the dark. Maybe, that's how it was for Job. Marcel Proust said, 'We are healed of a suffering only by experiencing it to the full.' I believe he's right. In the next two chapters I look at how we are invited to be with our grief and to experience our pain before we can know something new.

Waiting in the Darkness and the Absence

Journeys of waiting and unfulfillment are necessary if we seek fulfilment in God. They are an integral part of our grief walk. The day between Good Friday and Easter Day is given over to waiting; waiting in the dark. This is called Holy Saturday. It's a place and time where we hang in limbo, waiting for something to happen, questioning and doubting, knowing that we are powerless to influence the outcome. Holy Saturday has about it a sense of abandonment.

It's easy to skip over Holy Saturday; after all, we know how the story ends. So we fast-forward through the pain on Good Friday and the inactivity of Holy Saturday to the joy and triumph of Easter Day. Holy Saturday may seem like a boring day, but it's the day that was made for those of us who are grieving.

The disciples thought it was all over. They had no understanding of Jesus' resurrection. What will happen to his message? Was Jesus who he said he was? Who they thought he was? Have the authorities won and successfully buried him? When Jesus died they experienced the death of a close friend, and that was bad enough, but it was also the death of all their hopes and expectations. I put myself into the disciples' place and wonder what they were feeling and thinking: fear, frustration, anger, depression, and doubt, much doubt. Where is God?

The Easter Walk

Christians are given to interpreting loss and grief in the light of resurrection, overlooking the two preceding days. We are unfamiliar with the need to wait in this uncomfortable place. Caleb Wilde, who as a funeral director is very familiar with this time of waiting, muses on this dynamic.

> But skipping ahead to Easter might be what makes so many believers so unfamiliar with the pain, silence and doubt of death. If there's one reason why believers use comfort clichés – like, 'you'll see him again someday,' 'She's in a better place,' 'God doesn't give you more than you can handle.' 'Heaven will wipe away all your tears' – it's because they've only read the resurrection chapter of the story, and they've used that chapter as a shield against the darkness of death and anxiety.[130]

On our Holy Saturdays it seems God is absent, or at least elusive. The Welsh priest-poet R. S. Thomas wrote about the absence of God: 'Never known as anything / but as an absence, I dare not name him / as God.'[131] Yet, in this absence there is a presence.

> In this great absence
> that is like a presence, that compels
> me to address it without hope
> of a reply. It is a room I enter
>
> from which someone has just
> gone, the vestibule for the arrival
> of one who has not yet come.[132]

In this great absence we wait and fling out our questions. Perhaps there's no hope of a reply. Yet the fact we still pose our questions suggests, as it did for the psalmist and Job, that somehow, somewhere, God may yet respond.

Grief is a journey across a terrain that can be dark and fearful and, quite naturally, we want to skip it. But we can't do that, or at least, not

---

[130] Caleb Wilde, *Confessions of a Funeral Director – How the Business of Death Saved My Life* (New York: Harper Collins, 2017), 115–116.
[131] R. S. Thomas, 'Adjustments' in *Collected Poems 1945-1990* (Phoenix, London, 1990), 345.
[132] Thomas, 'The Absence' in *Collected Poems*, 361.

The Grief Walk

if we wish to travel to a place where something new can be found. We must wait in the darkness. In the Easter story we can't escape the darkness of Good Friday. Matthew names it.

> From noon on, darkness came over the whole land until three in the afternoon. And about three o'clock Jesus cried with a loud voice, 'Eli, Eli, lema sabachthani?' that is, 'My God, my God, why have you forsaken me?' (27:45)

In the darkness Jesus knows the great absence; he knows what it is to be forsaken by God. The darkness remains through Saturday and is there on the morning of Easter Day. We can't sidestep the darkness and rush on to the light of Easter Day, and John the Gospel writer ensures that we don't. He begins his account of Easter Day, 'Early on the first day of the week, *while it was still dark*' (20:1).

The gospel hope in the face of loss and grief is rooted in the belief that new life is discovered in the dark places of human existence. 'While it was still dark.' While it was still dark, Mary Magdalene went to the tomb, and stood there weeping. She has lost the most important person in her life: 'They have taken away my Lord, and I do not know where they have laid him' (20:2). It was a double grief. Not only had her beloved friend and teacher died, but also his body was gone, and she couldn't even spend a few minutes with it mourning.

There's a poignant reality about John's account of Easter morning because we know what it is to experience loss. Like Mary we have woken up to the darkness of grief because someone we love has died, because a hope we held dear has been shattered, because a relationship has ended, because we have no work to go to, because our familiar world no longer exists. Grief always begins in a place of darkness; the darkness that Jesus knew on Good Friday.

It's only natural to want to move on from the darkness and the waiting and stand in the light of Easter morning, but we aren't ready to encounter Easter morning until we have spent time waiting in the dark place where we cannot see hope. Easter is about hope in the midst of darkness. It's about meeting the risen Jesus in the dark places of our lives.

Grieving the death of his son, Richard Lischer read Psalm 139. He had noticed that in most of the psalms the figure of God is bathed in light, but this psalm strays from that imagery and invites us to imagine that light and darkness are the same to God: 'even the darkness is not dark to you; the night is as bright as the day, for darkness is as light to you' (139:12).

> If true, it means that God is capable of working in the dark. Which means that healing begins where creation began: in chaos and darkness. God doesn't wait until the depression lifts or spiritual adjustments have been made before he begins to stir in the human heart.[133]

I'm left wondering if real hope can only be born in darkness. If this is so, then we must allow ourselves to be in the darkness and allow darkness to be darkness. It means that we must learn to wait in the darkness, giving our eyes the time to adjust to it. It means that we must face the harsh fact of our pain and loss, face the new reality that we never wanted. This is an essential aspect of the grief walk. Then, in time, hints of resurrection appear.

Gradual, Imperceptible Resurrection

Resurrection isn't something that only belongs to the past or future. It's to be found in the present, in what's happening to us now. This is the gift of Easter morning. With the dawn may come something new: new hope, new alternatives, new beginnings. Resurrection is to be experienced in the present stuff of life, including the grief we are presently undergoing.

There are enough inspirational grief stories out there that present an unrealistic ideal. They are unhelpful because they imply that the pain will go away and the grief will vanish. Even as the days get better, the pain of grief remains in some form for a long time, perhaps for the rest of our lives. When I speak of resurrection, I'm not propounding a belief that I think will banish our pain. It may not, probably will not, even soothe it. Rather, it's a creative power which, somehow, transforms our pain and grief. Resurrection is about unearthing

---

[133] Lischer, *Stations of the Heart*, 234.

The Grief Walk

hope in the toughest and most chaotic places and uncovering a new life within our broken-heartedness.

The key to resurrection is not to be preoccupied with it, because it happens imperceptibly. Its coming is usually gradual and imperceptible. The creative work of resurrection transpires over time, maybe a lifetime. We tend to see it in the rear-vision mirror as we look back and see how we have changed. Not infrequently, we are not the one to see the changes. We need others who know us well to point them out to us. New life and transformation emerge in small, subtle ways. God's workings, the divine stirrings in the heart, are seldom dramatic. They are usually very unassuming, at least for those of us who are grieving. Grief isn't characterised by sudden or dramatic reversals; it doesn't 'break' like a fever.

For resurrection to have any real meaning, we must return to Good Friday and Holy Saturday; return to the place of pain and enter into it. This is contrary to all our natural instincts. We want to bypass pain and be relieved of it. It's a reason why many people have turned funerals into celebrations, sanitising the past and erasing anything that may hurt. It's why we are afraid to even use the words death and grief. It frightens us. It confronts us with our suffering and forces us to face the darkness we are experiencing. But if we jump straight into Easter morning and proclaim resurrection without spending time in those preceding days, seeking to evade the pain, then we deny ourselves the opportunity to continue the walk that may take us to a new place where our grief may become something other than a curse to be avoided at all costs.

Resurrection reveals the light of God within the darkest night. It's a gradual, subtle, inconspicuous work of God and the place of waiting, our Holy Saturday, is a place that we may well have to return to many times. Pierre Teilhard de Chardin, a Jesuit palaeontologist, geologist, and philosopher wrote of the need to 'trust in the slow work of God.' We are, he said, 'quite naturally impatient in everything to reach the end without delay.'

> We should like to skip the intermediate stages.
> We are impatient of being on the way to something
> unknown, something new.
> And yet it is the law of all progress
> that it is made by passing through
> some stages of instability –
> and that it may take a very long time.

He concludes his prayerful reflection:

> Give Our Lord the benefit of believing
> that his hand is leading you,
> and accept the anxiety of feeling yourself
> in suspense and incomplete.[134]

---

[134] Pierre Teilhard de Chardin, 'Patient Trust' in *Hearts on Fire: Praying with Jesuits,* ed. Michael Harter (Chicago: Loyola Press, 1993), 102.

12 – A Choice – Do we go Through the Pain or Around it?

Significant grief rarely, if ever, leaves us unchanged. It's not so much what happens to us but how we choose to respond. As we negotiate our grief walk, we come to various junctures where we are presented with a choice: to either enter the pain or seal it off, to go through it or around it. I don't say this lightly, for I know only too well that entering our pain can be frightening. Will it overwhelm me? Will I ever emerge from it? What might it do to me? And yes, it's tempting to numb the pain with distractions, with noise, pills, alcohol, or activity. We can't live with the intensity of the pain all the time. We move in and out of it, but the fundamental choice remains: how do we choose to respond?

We have good reason to deny or minimise our losses for grieving is painful. It takes immense energy and can open us to other unacknowledged losses. Grief leaves us feeling vulnerable, and that's frightening. So we may choose to do anything to make life the same as it was before the loss. We bury our grief and pretend the world is the same as it always was. And, in time the pain may diminish, and we get on with life, but we have denied ourselves the opportunity for healing and transformation. It's only if we are able to name and acknowledge our losses, to stay with the pain, and to embrace it, that our grief becomes less scary and less damaging to others and ourselves and can become a place of grace.

> Grief invites us to stand at the intersection of human and divine, stripped of ourselves, vulnerable to moments of grace. But it takes courage to stand at the corner and recognise the cross before us, etched unexpectedly into the road we are on.[135]

It does take courage because it leaves us vulnerable and our culture doesn't cope well with vulnerability. It's why people want to fix us and

---

135 Slevcove, *Broken Hallelujahs*, 200–201.

A Choice – Do we go Through the Pain or Around it?

get us back to normal as quickly as possible. It's why we are attracted to models of grief that explain it all so neatly in predictable stages, and why, like Job's friends, we offer tidy theological answers or the latest remedy presented on social media. But when we are grieving this drives us back into hiding, so we need a trustworthy companion, perhaps a support group, or sometimes a trained professional, to accompany us on this walk; people who can accept and bear witness to our pain; who will sit with us on our mourning bench. Rabbi Matthew Gewirtz describes what this might mean.

> We cry and yell out and accept the support our community wants to send our way. We allow ourselves to lash out in anger and frustration at the world and even, and especially, at God. We allow ourselves to be weak in ways we learned we were not supposed to. We become vulnerable and deeply open because all we want to do is tell our truth since it hurts too much to keep it inside. We allow ourselves to feel small and insignificant in this huge world and thus begin to feel relief because it isn't all about us. We allow transformation, even though it is frightening to confront certain parts of ourselves that we haven't quite wanted to see. We do what is counterintuitive and show the world that to expose our weaknesses is to eventually find our deepest strength. We can transform; we can transcend; but first we must have the fortitude to surrender to our reality.[136]

Stewards of our Pain

Frederick Buechner, writer and theologian, talks about our stewardship of pain – that is, the different ways in which we deal with the sad, painful, and puzzling things that happen to us over the course of our lives.

Depending on the day, depending on how we are feeling, we respond differently to our pain, but Frederick suggests there are some basic alternatives that we can choose from. The most appealing is to forget

---

[136] Matthew Gewirtz, 'The Gift of Grief: Finding Peace, Transformation, and Renewed Life After Great Sorrow.' Accessed from:
http://www.spiritualityandpractice.com/books/reviews/excerpts/view/18145

The Grief Walk

the pain, to shut it away, to pretend it never happened, because it's too hard to deal with and too unsettling to remember. This is a common response, especially from those of us who learned to keep a stiff upper lip, not to complain, and never to talk about things that hurt. Grief, therefore, like any pain, is kept hidden; hidden from others and hidden from ourselves. But there's a price to be paid for pushing our pain aside. The price is that in some way we don't grow, denying ourselves the possibility of discovering something new. Frederick's mother lived to be almost 92 and became quite adept at burying her pain. She remained a very valuable, interesting person, but the development of a certain part of her was arrested.

> I think the part of her that didn't grow was what might have been her compassionate part of her, the part of her that by looking at her own pain would have opened her up to the sense that others were in pain, and then she might have been able to reach out into other people's lives. She never did… The human part of her that might have been never really came to be because of all the things she sort of stuffed aside, the things that might have opened her.[137]

Another response is to become embittered and trapped in our grief. A classic example of this is the character of Miss Havisham in Charles Dickens' novel *Great Expectations*. Her bridegroom jilted her on her wedding day, and that was the end of her life. She spent the rest of her days sitting in the room where the great reception was to have been, her wedding cake mouldering, her dress long since turned to rags, imprisoned in a sadness that she never could escape. For Miss Havisham, her grief became her confinement.

> You keep living it over and over and over again, almost relishing the bitterness of it. So you deal with your pain by allowing it to overwhelm you, by allowing it to stop you in your tracks. And I suppose it's also a way of surviving your pain, because as in the case of Miss Havisham, you take a kind of grim, awful pleasure in your ruin.[138]

---

[137] Frederick Buechner, *A Crazy, Holy Grace: The Healing power of Pain and Memory* (Grand Rapids, Michigan: Zondervan, 2017), 32.
[138] Buechner, *A Crazy, Holy Grace*, 33.

A Choice – Do we go Through the Pain or Around it?

Another way is to make a joke of the loss, to make light of it. A woman told Frederick the deeply sad story of her marriage. Her husband had been diagnosed with premature dementia. He had lost all sense of judgement and would disappear for days on end. They had lost all their money and their various creditors were suing them. She had finally divorced her husband though she was still living with him.

> It's just a hopeless story… But as she told it, she kept laughing this awful, chill, unearthly, inhuman laugh, as if her way of surviving her pain was to make a kind of joke out of it: 'Guess what's happened to me, and guess what all has come about?' It made it almost impossible to talk to her seriously about these terrible things because, in a way, she was holding them off… She made a joke of it. She hid her pain behind the joke.[139]

Other options include competitive pain: 'You think you've had it bad? Wait 'till you've heard what's happened to me!' Pain becomes a kind of accomplishment. Or using the pain as an excuse for failure: 'If these terrible things hadn't happened to me – if I hadn't suffered these rotten losses – who knows what I might've become or done.'

These are all survival techniques that diminish us. I don't think we consciously choose to employ them, but they are responses we may have acquired in childhood from our family, or perhaps learned from our surrounding culture. An alternative way of responding to our pain is to be a good steward of it. This is about remaining in touch with our grief, entering it, embracing it, and allowing it to be a part who we are. Frederick Buechner offers this thought-provoking observation about our experiences of pain.

> I think it is often those times when we were most alive, when we were somehow closest to being most vitally human beings. Keep in touch with it because it is at those moments of pain where you are most open to the pain of other people – most open to your own deep places. Keep in touch with those sad times because it is then that you are most aware of your own powerlessness, crushed in a way by what is

---

139 Buechner, *A Crazy, Holy Grace*, 35.

> happening to you, but also most aware of God's power to pull you through it, to be with you in it. Keeping in touch with your pain, I think, means also to be true to who in your depths you have it in you to be – depths of pain and also in a way depths of joy, because they both come from the same place.[140]

When we push our pain away, when we try to bury it and pretend it's not there, we ultimately yield to its death-making process and lead a diminished life, as did Miss Havisham and Frederick's mother. When we enter our pain, rather than circumventing it, we allow resurrection to be a real possibility. Our pain becomes a path towards transformation and the discovery of something new.

This approach to the pain of our grief is paradoxical. The wounding of our grief can become a blessing. The verb *to wound* in French is *blesser*. Phillip Bennett says this tells us that:

> When we have gone into the pain, instead of running from it, we discover new hope and compassion which has been forged in the fire of suffering. To the degree that we have embraced our pain, we, like Jesus, have descended into hell, have gone all the way down into our darkness and despair and have come out the other side into the resurrection life.
>
> The words 'wound' and 'wonder' share a common root which means to 'penetrate.' Our wounds are the places where life has penetrated us. These places can become either infected and closed off or they can become channels that open us to fuller life and love.[141]

I'm not suggesting that God gives us these experiences, or as people sometimes say, 'there's a reason for your loss.' Grief, like any suffering, is painful. This doesn't mean, however, that we deny the truth that the experience of suffering may in some way transform us. But we can only know this if we choose to travel *through* the pain rather than sidestepping it.

---

140 Frederick Buechner, 'Stewardship of Pain'. Accessed from https://searchingforfaith.blogs.com/on_a_pilgrimage/2005/02/stewardship-of-pain-frederick-buechner.html
141 Bennett, *Let Yourself Be Loved*, 15.

A Choice – Do we go Through the Pain or Around it?

To speak of life out of death, hope out of despair, is a mystery, one that stands at the heart of the gospel; and, like many mysteries, it contains tension. Nicholas Wolterstorff struggled to hold this tension after his son's death.

> Suffering may do us good – may be a blessing, something to be thankful for. This I have learned… Suffering is the shout of 'No' by one's whole existence to that over which one suffers – the shout of 'No' by nerves and gut and gland and heart to pain, to death, to injustice, to depression, to hunger, to humiliation, to bondage, to abandonment. And sometimes, when the cry is intense, there emerges a radiance which elsewhere seldom appears: a glow of courage, of love, of insight, of selflessness, of faith. In that radiance we see best what humanity was meant to be.[142]

But then, Nicholas wonders, how can this be; how can he thank God for this radiance while at the same time asking for its removal.

> In the valley of suffering, despair and bitterness are brewed. But there also character is made. The valley of suffering is the vale of soul-making. But now things slip and slide around… For what do I give thanks and for what do I lament?… How do I sustain my 'No' to my son's early death while accepting with gratitude the opportunity offered of becoming what otherwise I could never be?[143]

New life discovered after a significant loss contains a tension between the realities of what we have lost and what we have found. They don't, in my experience, fit together in some neat pattern of divine purpose. They just are and the tension remains. That said, we have a choice: do we enter the pain and become good stewards of it, or do we ignore it?

To enter the depths of our grief is a risky venture. We can never be sure of what we will find. We may encounter within its depths forgotten and hidden monsters as well as pearls of great price. But it seems to me that what we do uncover is our true self, each other, and God who is present with us in our pain.

---

142 Wolterstorff, *Lament for a Son*, 96
143 Wolterstorff, *Lament for a Son*, 97.

A Great Freedom – How do we Respond?

There is much in life that we have no control over. Losses usually come unbidden, but we can always retain one fundamental freedom that we can exercise. From the sufferings of the concentration camps Viktor Frankl found that this is the last and greatest of freedoms: to choose how we will respond.

> We who lived in concentration camps can remember the men who walked through the huts comforting others, giving away their last piece of bread. They may have been few in number, but they offer sufficient proof that everything can be taken from a man but the one thing: the last of the human freedoms – to choose one's attitude in any given set of circumstances, to choose one's own way.
>
> And there were always choices to make. Every day, every hour, offered the opportunity to make a decision which determined whether you would or would not submit to those powers which threaten to rob you of your very self, your inner freedom; which determined whether or not you would become the plaything of circumstance...[144]

Viktor's conclusion is that the sort of person we become, emotionally and mentally, is 'the result of an inner decision' and not the consequence of circumstances alone. Faced with our loss we have a choice: how do we choose to respond?

The *why* question is not uncommon in grief: 'Why did this happen?' 'Why not them?' It's a big question because it expresses our primal need for meaning. But there comes a time when we begin to ask *what* and *how* questions: 'What can I do with this unwanted situation?' 'What do I need to do to make sense of all this?' 'How do I live with this new reality?' 'How can I be in this?' 'How do I choose to respond?' Then the *where* question emerges: 'Where is God in this?' This progression of questions takes time, but it offers a way forward to something new.

---

144 Frankl, *Man's Search for Meaning*, 62.

A Choice – Do we go Through the Pain or Around it?

Our willingness to ask the *where* question is shaped by how we see God. To believe in the God of suffering love who is *with* us means that we don't have to go searching for God. We don't have to plead for God to be present. God is already present. Our task is to recognise that presence and to ask, how might I respond? God is 'like a person who clears his throat while hiding and so gives himself away. God lies in wait for us with nothing so much as love,' said Meister Eckhart.

13 – Our Search for Meaning after Loss

Moving Grief from a Noun to a Verb

Much of the literature on loss and grief limits its understanding of grief to a personal *reaction* to loss, discussing how we 'go through' grief. This is a passive approach which can leave us in a victim mode. But grief is also about our *response*. Our grief reactions are not a matter of choice, but our response is.

Seeing grief as an active response is one of the changes of thinking that's occurred in recent years. It moves our experience of grief from being a noun to being a verb. This dynamic involves what is referred to as 'meaning reconstruction,' which resonates with our Christian journey, for any healthy spirituality or belief structure seeks to show us ways of responding creatively to pain and suffering, loss and grief.

What is Meaning?

> 'Who are *you*?' said the Caterpillar... Alice replied, rather shyly, 'I – I hardly know, sir, just at present – at least I know who I *was* when I got up this morning, but I think I must have been changed several times since then.'[145]

The questions we ask – the whys and wheres, the hows and whats – point to the most fundamental challenge we face when we lose what we love, when we lose what is significant to us. These questions, to borrow Viktor Frankl's line, are about 'our search for meaning.'

But what does *meaning* mean? Meaning is about the big stuff in life. We touch on meaning when we ask questions like, 'Who am I?' 'Why me?' 'What's the point of it all?' 'What do I now do with my life?' 'How do I make sense of what's happened?' 'Where is God in this?' 'Where do I go from here?' 'Who is God?' 'Does God exist, and if God does exist where does God fit into my experience?' Our responses to such

---

[145] Lewis Carroll, *Alice's Adventures in Wonderland* (London: Macmillan and Co., 1866), 60.

questions are expressions of meaning. Melissa Kelley helps unpack the word.

> From the German root *meinen*, which is 'to think,' meaning is the deep sense we make of things, the way we understand the world, how we articulate the overarching purpose or goal of our lives, the significance we seek in living, the core values by which we order our lives. Meaning also includes theological dimensions such as how we understand God's activity in the world, God's feelings about and responses to us, and God's role in suffering.
>
> Meaning, including theological meaning, helps to create order, sense, and purpose out of experiences and events that could otherwise seem random, nonsensical, disordered, or chaotic.[146]

Without meaning, our lives become fragmented and frightening, lacking a sense of order, purpose, and wholeness. Meaninglessness can lead to death, if not physically, then emotionally. Viktor Frankl quotes the German philosopher Friedrich Nietzsche: 'He who has a *why* to live for can bear with almost any *how*,' and goes on to say:

> Woe to him who saw no more sense in his life, no aim, no purpose, and therefore no point in carrying on. He was soon lost. The typical reply with which such a man rejected all encouraging arguments was, 'I have nothing to expect from life any more.' What sort of answer can one give to that?[147]

Reconstructing our Meaning after Loss

Following a loss, our sense of meaning can be thrown into disarray. We think, 'I know where I'm going, and I know who is going with me,' except that when we lose a person we love, we no longer know where we are going or who is going with us. We think, 'I know the purpose of my life,' except we lose our job, or we are incapacitated, and the purpose we have constructed for ourselves is suddenly deconstructed.

---

146 Kelley, *Grief: Contemporary Theory and the Practice of Ministry*, 75.
147 Frankl, *Man's Search for Meaning*, 72.

The Grief Walk

Sometimes our sense of meaning can accommodate a loss without being dislocated. That doesn't mean how we see life isn't changed in some way, but the essential meaning remains intact. For instance, both my parents died following lingering illnesses, and there was a real sense of relief and release. I certainly grieved for them, and over time I learned to reinterpret my life story, but their deaths didn't threaten my sense of meaning. In contrast, a loss can threaten the meaning we have established for ourselves so that it no longer makes sense. Our meaning and purpose, for example, may have been tied up with our marriage. We envisaged a long marriage, including children and grandchildren. But then our marriage is ended by an unanticipated divorce or by sudden death. Or we found our meaning in our job, but then we are seriously disabled and no longer able to work. The purpose we gave to our lives is challenged, even demolished. No wonder a common response to a major loss is the statement, 'This doesn't make sense.' The meaning we gave to our lives has gone. At its core, grief as a verb seeks to affirm or reconstruct a personal meaning that has been changed and challenged by the loss.

Reconstructing our meaning is a gradual process that takes place over time. It's rather like rewriting or editing the story of our lives. The narrative we had planned has to be reimagined and reworked. As we grieve, we tend to tell and retell the story of our loss. If we listen carefully to the telling and retelling, we will notice that the story, or at least the way we tell the story, gradually changes, for what we are doing is reshaping our story: finding new understanding and meaning, purpose and hope. That's why it's important to have people who can listen to our telling and retelling and who can ask open and perceptive questions and help us reflect on our experience. These are people who will encourage us to talk as much as we need to talk; who will be with us and listen. Our faith community, because of our shared spirituality, ought to be a place where such telling and listening can go on. Another place where we might tell and listen is with those who have known parallel experiences of loss. Provided that it's recognised that we grieve uniquely, these are people who can have a particular empathy for others who have known comparable losses.

Any experience can be interpreted in different ways. Think of the perennial question, 'Is the glass half full or half empty?' The same glass may be seen in two quite different ways, and each view suggests a different meaning. We interpret our experiences out of our own understanding. As a well-known expression puts it, 'We don't see things as they are. We see them as we are.' When any aspect of our self-understanding changes, new interpretations may arise, and new interpretations make possible new meanings.

The meanings we construct for ourselves express our sense of purpose, values, beliefs, and priorities. They say what is important and valuable to us. While the process of reconstructing our meaning after a loss can be painful and painstaking, it can also be an opportunity to review what really matters to us, what gives us life; and to discover new insights. This may result in giving up meanings that are unhelpful, even destructive.

Our meaning doesn't drop out of the sky. Some of our meaning-making is very conscious as we make choices along the way. Other meanings we acquire or assimilate from others, such as family, religion, or surrounding culture, and it's not uncommon for people who have experienced a loss to rid themselves of meanings that are no longer life-giving. This takes us back to how we see God. I asked earlier, what kind of God do we have? How do we understand God? In the light of our loss, how do we relate to God and how does God respond to us? Where is God in all this? These are questions that Nicholas Wolterstorff and C. S. Lewis asked with brutal candidness. As we ask such questions, we are delving into the deepest understandings of life, seeking meaning as we adjust to the new normal that the loss has imposed upon us.

Different understandings of God lead to different meanings. Our idea of God can shape whether we live in hopeful meaning or desperate meaninglessness after loss. Sometimes the meanings we have acquired have very harmful consequences. Some expressions of Christianity encourage women to stay in abusive marriages because it's deemed God prohibits divorce. This view implies that God sanctions violence and abuse over the dissolution of a marriage and suggests a picture of a punishing, terrifying, even sadistic god.

The Grief Walk

Melissa Kelly rightly asks:

> What sorts of meanings might this God concept yield? How will abused women and children understand their worth and dignity? How will they imagine their futures? What will they believe about their value in God's eyes? … Will they ultimately live in hopeful meaning or desperate meaninglessness?[148]

The same could be said of people who are same-gender attracted or gender diverse. These people may have been subjected to abuse and exclusion by family members and faith communities, much of which is 'justified' by a certain understanding or perception of God.

Some people are unable either to affirm or to rebuild meaning after a loss, and find themselves in a state of meaninglessness, lacking any sense of purpose or direction in their lives. Life becomes pointless and existence is random and disconnected. It's a desolate condition, though sadly it's far from unknown. When I witness this state, it drives me back to what matters most of all. While grief is commonly seen through the lens of psychology, my response is ultimately in terms of relationship: with God, with others, and with ourselves. In other words, it's a theological and spiritual response, for we all have a god or gods, even the professed atheist. After all, our god is what we place our trust in and is our ultimate source of meaning.

Meaning in Love

> A thought transfixed me: for the first time in my life I saw the truth… that love is the ultimate and highest goal to which man can aspire. Then I grasped the meaning of the greatest secret that human poetry and human thought and belief have to impart: *The salvation of man is through love and in love.* I understood how a man who has nothing left in this world still may know bliss, be it only for a moment, in the contemplation of his beloved… For the first time in my life I was able to understand the meaning of the words, 'The angels are lost in perpetual contemplation of the infinite glory.'[149]

---

148 Kelley, *Grief: Contemporary Theory and the Practice of Ministry*, 88.
149 Frankl, *Man's Search for Meaning*, 35–36.

Our Search for Meaning after Loss

In this reflection Viktor Frankl is thinking primarily of his love for his wife, though it could well be applied to God who is Love: the ultimate meaning in our lives. The way we see and understand God leads to different meanings. The spiritual writer Thomas Merton articulates something of the meaning on which I base my life.

> To say that I am made in the image of God is to say that love is the reason for my existence, for God is love. Love is my true identity. Selflessness is my true self. Love is my true character. Love is my name.[150]

Love is who God is; love is what we are called to be. I therefore find meaning in love. This includes my experiences of loss and grief.

Many of our questions may go unanswered, for there is so much we cannot understand. We might call this mystery; what we experience but cannot understand; what we apprehend but cannot comprehend. At the heart of the Christian story is the mystery of God's love shown through the life, suffering, death, and resurrection of Jesus. Paul, pondering the suffering we experience, asks, 'What then are we to say about these things?' He answers his own question by affirming the mystery of divine love.

> No, in all these things we are more than conquerors through him who loved us. For I am convinced that neither death, nor life, nor angels, nor rulers, nor things present, nor things to come, nor powers, nor height, nor depth, nor anything else in all creation, will be able to separate us from the love of God in Christ Jesus our Lord. (Romans 8:31a, 37-39)

There is a paradox in all this. There is suffering and pain, *and* God is love. We know loss and grief from the day we are born, *and* God is love. The Christian faith offers no promise that we will be spared pain and suffering, only the assurance that nothing 'will be able to separate us from the love of God in Christ Jesus.' This doesn't deny the harsh reality of grief. We grieve for what we have loved and lost, but we need not be plunged into the despair of meaninglessness. 'We are tethered' as Melissa Kelley puts it, 'in an ultimate sense to a

---

150 Thomas Merton, *New Seeds of Contemplation* (New York: New Directions, 1961), 30.

loving, cherishing God who holds us and protects us from the threat of meaninglessness.'[151]

To be tethered to God who is love or, using an image I offered earlier, to know God as our ultimate attachment and secure base, gives us a fundamental sense of trust and security that enables us to explore this changed world that we now inhabit.

Living in a Changed World

> Change and loss, Dilys said to herself, like a chant, over and over, life carrying you away, carrying things away from you, then bringing something back, some little thing you didn't look for, didn't know you needed until you saw it washed up there, waiting at your feet. Change and loss. And growth. Growth where you had never looked for it before, never thought to look. Because you weren't ready. Because you hadn't known the loss.[152]

Grief is a painful process of change, by which we gradually give up one world and enter another. The world that we occupy following loss is foreign. Loss breaks our hearts, it may challenge our meaning, and it certainly changes our reality. Reflecting on his life after the death of his brother, Frederick Buechner described how his world had changed in a profound way.

> There is a level that I know nothing about at all except that whatever I am doing there, it is absolutely exhausting. It is as if great quantities of furniture have to be moved from one place to another. There seems to be endless cartons of God only knows what to sort through somehow. The earth itself has to be bulldozed and shifted around and reshaped. A whole new landscape has to come into being.[153]

We didn't ask for this new landscape; it wasn't on our itinerary, but that's where we find ourselves. Grief isn't like the flu. We don't recover

---

151 Kelley, *Grief: Contemporary Theory and the Practice of Ministry*, 90.
152 Trollope, *Next of Kin*, 248.
153 Frederick Buechner, *The Eyes of the Heart: A Memoir of the Lost and Found* (New York: HarperCollins, 1999), 147.

from it and go back to how things were before the loss. Grief changes us, but the changes that take place need not be for the worse. On the contrary, out of the fire of grief we can know transformation and discover something new.

> When we experience loss – of a loved one, of health, of a job, a familiar way of life – the pain is tremendous. There is no way to short-circuit our grief; it comes in waves which only gradually lessen in intensity… But over time our loss begins to give us hidden riches: a gratitude for every precious moment of life; a sense that all is a gift to be treasured; a deepened empathy for others. These are not riches we have chosen; they, like our losses, have come unbidden, unexpectedly… As we find new depths of meaning even while we still ache with loss, others begin to see the riches in us; they recognise in us someone who has suffered and so can understand their losses without giving words of false comfort.[154]

The change we experience is not only in how our world looks, but also in us. Some people will respond with ongoing bitterness, cynicism, and anger; becoming like Miss Havisham, imprisoned in their grief, while others will ultimately find new life within this change by continuing to grow and learn. When Nicholas Wolterstorff was asked whether he had changed, he replied:

> The suffering of the world has worked its way deeper inside me… Each person's suffering has its own quality. No outsider can ever fully enter it. Yet more of suffering is now accessible to me… And I now know about helplessness – of what to do when there is nothing to do.[155]

Later Nicholas articulated what he hoped for from living with grief: that sympathy for the world's wounds be enlarged by our anguish; love for those around be expanded; gratitude for what is good might flame up; insight be deepened; and commitment to what is important be strengthened.[156]

---

154 Bennett, *Let Yourself Be Loved*, 33–34.
155 Wolterstorff, *Lament for a Son*, 72.
156 Wolterstorff, *Lament for a Son*, 92.

The Grief Walk

Joanne Guy, whose son Scott was murdered in his driveway on his way to milk the cows, describes how their family made the choice early on to 'find new purpose and meaning in life even after terrible heartbreak.'

> For a long time I tried to find my way back, only to discover that I never was going to! There is no way back to our old lives and the way we viewed the world… A crisis makes us look at how we live our lives. We start seeing things differently. We stop and re-evaluate.
>
> My perspective has completely changed. It is like having new lenses on my eyes. Time is my most valued commodity. Time spent with family and loved ones and slowing down enough to enjoy what I have today. I take nothing for granted. Tomorrow may never come. The beauty of nature holds me spellbound. To me I can see God's hand and feel a deep peace. I listen more to the yearnings of my soul. I appreciate the still and quiet.
>
> I have become more aware of others around me who are suffering. I care deeply for kids who can't find their way because of the big issues and losses in their lives. It motivates me to write and visit schools. To be a lighthouse.
>
> I look at the things I can do and decide what is important to me and live for that. I am still learning and changing, and I am on a creative mission this year of doing new things. I am even going back to drawing, among other things. Creativity is so important in our healing process.
>
> So whatever place you are in with your grieving, try not to be impatient. As the world carries on around you and it feels like your world has stopped you will find everything has a season. You will find your way.[157]

Joanne echoes Viktor Frankl who concluded that the greatest task in our lives is to find meaning. Viktor saw three possible sources

---

157 Joanne Guy, 'Forever Changed.' Accessed from https://www.makelemonade.co.nz/2018/03/14/changed/

for meaning: in work (doing something significant), in love (caring for another person), and in courage during difficult times. I add a fourth: encountering the life and love and God.

Suffering in and of itself is meaningless, but we give our suffering meaning by the way in which we respond to it. Joanne found that she couldn't go back. So much had changed. She had changed. Joanne chose to look to the future; to give to others, especially those grieving; to find new creativity. Meaninglessness takes hold of us when we lock ourselves into the past, but as Viktor Frankl asserted, a future with a goal gives hope. Without a future we tend to focus on the past to make the pain of the present less real. But Viktor warned, if we rob the present of its reality, we are in danger of overlooking the opportunities that the present, however painful it may be, contains. If we immerse ourselves in a retrospective view of life, we deny ourselves the possibility of discovering something new. 'Such people forgot that often it is just such an exceptionally difficult external situation which gives man the opportunity to grow spiritually beyond himself.'[158] We gain inner strength by focusing our lives on a future goal.

> It is a peculiarity of man that he can only live by looking to the future – *sub specie aeternitatis* [under the aspect of eternity]. And this is his salvation in the most difficult moments of his existence, although he sometimes has to force his mind to the task.[159]

I have pinned to my study wall the words, 'You are never too old to set another goal or to dream a new dream.' I could reframe that: 'Whatever I lose, I can still set another goal and dream a new dream.' How we live that out, how we undertake these tasks and seek meaning, is as unique to each of us as is our grief. But I have learned, as Viktor asserts, it cannot be something vague; it must be very real and concrete.

It takes courage and hope to dream a new dream after a major loss. But eventually we need to take the steps to engage with the new

---

158 Frankl, *Man's Search for Meaning*, 67.
159 Frankl, *Man's Search for Meaning*, 68.

The Grief Walk

world that we now inhabit. At first our steps will probably be small, tentative ones, and we may fall over many times, but ultimately, we learn to live in this changed reality.

14 – Hope Emerges

Vaclav Havel, playwright and former president of Czechoslovakia, said, 'Hope is not the same thing as optimism. It is not the conviction that something will turn out well, but the certainty that something makes sense, regardless of how it turns out.'[160]

Vaclav Havel's suggestion is that hope makes or remakes meaning of our experience. Hope grounds us in our deepest values and gives us a reason to continue our journey. It gives us the reason to live with the present chaos, to enter the pain, to traverse an unknown territory, and discover a new reality. Hope asserts that transformation can come through loss.

Hopes and Goals

Hope underlies our belief that we can, in some way, reconstruct meaning. Of hope Lucy Hone says:

> [It is] the fuel that fires us to move forward in the world. The word for the alternative – hopelessness – says it all. I experienced hopelessness for the first time when Abi died; I woke up one morning in that first week and was shocked to find myself thinking, 'I hate life.'... This was probably my bleakest moment.[161]

Over time kernels of hope began to emerge, growing from just a flicker to something more. Hope strengthened Lucy's resolve and determination to forge forward.

Following a significant loss, we can feel lost because what gave meaning to our lives has gone. There is no hope for the future and we may well say, as did Lucy, 'I hate life.' But what she began to do in response was to nurture new hope. She found, as have many others, including Viktor Frankl, that having goals and daring to dream new

---

160 Vaclav Havel, *Disturbing the Peace: A Conversation with Karel Hvizdala;* trans. by Paul Wilson (New York: Alfred A. Knopf, 1990), 181-182.
161 Hone, *What Abi Taught Us,* 87.

dreams nurture hope. This is what Joanne Guy also did: 'I look at the things I can do and decide what is important to me and live for that.' At first our hope may be rooted in the simple but all-essential goal of surviving each day, moving one step in front of the other. Then in time our goals are extended.

> These are not goals like meeting deadlines; they are more about identifying what's important to you – the things that you value. Doing so helps you focus where you put your energy, time and commitment, the things you chase, and the issues and complaints you let go.[162]

Lucy's understanding of hope is that it isn't a single entity, but that we have a collection of smaller hopes. I agree that hope finds expression in various goals and creative tasks. For Christians there's a fundamental hope that underlies all that we do and are.

Hope Isn't a Magic Potion

We aren't made to be like the ancient Stoics who applauded those who stood above passion and emotion and refrained from either rejoicing or crying. Jesus invited people to celebrate and dance. He also invited them to grieve and to weep. This is something that our faith communities need to reflect. There must be a place for lamentation as well as celebration, for sorrow as well as joy. The problem is, so many ignore lamentation and sorrow and only celebrate and rejoice. To hear a pastor exhorting a grieving congregation that they must not sorrow but celebrate is not only abusive of people's grief but flies in the face of what we witness in Scripture. Death may well be a release from suffering and the indignities that can accompany a lingering dying, but death is still awful. It can be a very bitter pill to swallow. We are separated from the one we love, and life will never be the same again. Grief is no respecter of belief. The long and exhausting journey of grief is as hard for Christians with a vital faith as it is for others.

William Coffin's son died. As a clergyperson, William received a flood of letters, many from clerical colleagues, 'a few of whom proved they knew their Bibles better than the human condition.'

---

162 Hone, *What Abi Taught Us*, 113.

> I know all the 'right' biblical passages, including 'Blessed are those who mourn,' and my faith is no house of cards; these passages are true, I know. But the point is this. While the words of the Bible are true, grief renders them unreal. The reality of grief is the absence of God – 'MY God, my God, why hast thou forsaken me?' The reality of grief is the solitude of pain, the feeling that your heart is in pieces, your mind's a blank, that 'there is no joy the world can give like that it takes away' (Lord Byron).
>
> That's why immediately after such a tragedy people must come to your rescue, people who only want to hold your hand, not to quote anybody or even say anything, people who simply bring food and flowers – the basics of beauty and life – people who sign letters simply, 'Your brokenhearted sister.' In other words, in my intense grief I felt some of my fellow reverends... were using comforting words of Scripture for self-protection, to pretty up a situation whose bleakness they simply couldn't face. But like God herself, Scripture is not around for anyone's protection, just for everyone's unending support.[163]

The hope of the gospel isn't a magic potion that eliminates pain and suffering any more than the resurrection is a magical filler of the hole left in our lives by the death of a loved one. Nicholas Wolterstorff says:

> It did not console me to be reminded of the hope of resurrection. If I had forgotten that hope, then it would indeed have brought light into my life to be reminded of it. But I did not think of death as a bottomless pit. I did not grieve as one who has no hope. Yet Eric is gone, here and now he is gone; now I cannot talk with him, now I cannot see him, now I cannot hug him, now I cannot hear his plans for the future. That is my sorrow. A friend said, 'Remember, he's in good hands.' I was deeply moved. But the reality does not put Eric back in my hands now. That's my grief. For that

---

163 William Sloane Coffin, 'Alex's Death,' in *The Collected Sermons of William Sloane Coffin: The Riverside Years, Vol. 2* (Louisville: KY: Westminster John Knox Press, 2008), 4.

grief, what consolation can there be other than having him back?[164]

These personal reflections serve as warnings; reminders that faith doesn't erase the harsh reality of grief. The loss remains all too real. Comfort does not abide in religious words. As we saw in the story of Job, comfort is first and foremost experienced in presence: being with another, sharing lament and listening. Yet, though our grieving may be one of the hardest things we have ever experienced, there comes a point when we glimpse hope. The grief contains a trust that somehow, at some point, we will come to a new place and discover new life beyond the devastation we presently feel.

> Those who trust in this way experience hope for the future, even though, in the freshness of their grief, they can scarcely imagine what that future might look like. As someone has reminded us, 'Even though we cannot see beyond the headlights we know that the road goes on.' That is what it means to have hope![165]

Our Sustaining Hope: If God is for us

The Christian hope is rooted in the knowledge that God is love; that God loves us, and even though we may not feel it, and may at times question it, this love 'has been poured into our hearts through the Holy Spirit' (Romans 5:5b). Paul, writing to the Christian community in Rome, unpacks what this hope means in the face of suffering. His view of hope is rooted in who God is, and for that reason, he says, it 'does not disappoint' (5:5a) because God is who God is, and that's what provides confidence in facing the future and engaging with this changed world, this new reality that we must now come to terms with.

Paul acknowledges that suffering and heartbreak is a given in life; we can't avoid it, but our hope enables us to see what we are presently experiencing in a new light. Paul's picture of hope is cosmic in scope. He envisions God transforming and making new all of creation, and

---

164 Wolterstorff, *Lament for a Son*, 31.
165 John T. Schwiebert, 'Grief and Hope'. Accessed from https://griefwatch.com/grief-and-hope

the future glory that awaits us is much greater than the suffering we are presently experiencing. This isn't a line we thrust before a person in the midst of raw grief, but in time, as we learn to live in our new world and seek to reconstruct meaning we may find strength in the certain hope that, however hard and painful life is, there lies before us the promise of a glorious future. It's a hope that persists in believing that, because God is love, life and love will have the last word. This doesn't mean that our losses cease to hurt or that suffering doesn't touch us. Far from it; our brokenness is not the end of our story and through God's creative love a new life, a transformation, can emerge from all the pieces.

I think of Vaclav Havel's comment that 'Hope is… the certainty that something makes sense, regardless of how it turns out.' Paul knows that our future is in God's hands, and that is the basis for his confidence and joy. The future gives meaning and purpose to the present and the past, and Paul's grand vision of the future glory is what leads to hope. Christian hope realises God's ability to transform the future from an unpromising, painful, chaotic present. It allows us to dream new dreams and set new goals.

Paul's vision of hope culminates in one of his most eloquent declarations. I've already cited it because it's central to appreciating who God is. In chapter 8 of his letter to the faith community in Rome Paul presents a prosecutor who poses a series of rhetorical questions to a defendant (the Christian), and each time the answer is in terms of what God has done for us in Christ. 'If God is for us, who is against us?' (8:31) God is on our side, and no one can undo that relationship. Any forces marshalled against us are nothing; they cannot prevail. The prosecutor has no case against us. 'He who did not withhold his own Son, but gave him up for all of us, will he not with him also give us everything else?' (8:32) The demonstration that God is on our side is the gift of Jesus. God has given us the very best: God's beloved Son. If God was willing to give us that, is there anything God would withhold from us? The answer is a resounding 'No!' And Paul goes on to ask, 'Who will separate us from the love of Christ? Will hardship, or distress, or persecution, or famine, or nakedness, or peril, or sword?' (8:34, 35) He replies, 'No, in all these things we are more than conquerors through him who loved us' (8:37).

> I am convinced that neither death, nor life, nor angels, nor rulers, nor things present, nor things to come, nor powers, nor height, nor depth, nor anything else in all creation, will be able to separate us from the love of God in Christ Jesus our Lord. (8:38–39)

The certainty of God's love, poured into our hearts by the Spirit, is the foundation of Christian hope, and it's why this hope never disappoints. There is no experience that we can undergo that has the power to frustrate God's care and love for us, not even death. God has known us from the first and set us on the path surrounded by divine love that will always be with us. John Donne, poet-priest, said that one of the best symbols of God is a circle, for a circle is endless; 'whom God loves, God loves to the end; and not only to the end, to their death, but to God's end, and God's end is, that God might love them still.'[166]

This is our ultimate hope. It's not a happy optimism that insists everything will turn out rosy, nor will it protect us from the pain of grief. It doesn't shut down our questions by explaining them away or supplying a ready-made answer. Rather, it's the conviction that God has not and will not let us go, that somehow we are bound to God who is suffering love; that we can live hopefully, knowing that our lives are embedded within God's all-encompassing intention to transform and renew all creation. The stories of our individual lives may not have the happy endings we dreamed of, but the greater and over-arching narrative of God's story does. In the end, love wins. Love will not be defeated. I don't pretend to comprehend this, but as C. S. Lewis wrote near the end of his journal, 'The best is perhaps what we understand least.'[167]

---

[166] 'Sermon on The Nativity – Preached Christmas Day, 1624' in Henry Alford, *The Works of John Donne* (London: John W. Parker, 1839), 27.
[167] Lewis, *A Grief Observed*, 59.

Selected Bibliography

Phillip Bennett, *Let Yourself Be Loved* (Mahwah, N. J: Paulist Press, 1997).

Frederick Buechner, *A Crazy, Holy Grace: The Healing power of Pain and Memory* (Grand Rapids, Michigan: Zondervan, 2017).

Frederick Buechner, *The Eyes of the Heart: A Memoir of the Lost and Found* (New York: HarperCollins, 1999).

Walter Brueggemann, *The Message of the Psalms: A Theological Commentary* (Minneapolis: Augsburg Press, 1984).

Marian Carter, *Dying to Live: A Theological and Practical Workbook on Death, Dying and Bereavement* (London, SCM, 2014).

Alise D. Chaffins, *Embracing Grief: Leaning Into Loss to Find Life* (U.S.A., Createspace, 2015).

Kenneth J. Doka, *Grief is a Journey: Finding your Path through Loss* (New York: Atria Books, 2016.

Kenneth J. Doka (ed.), *Disenfranchised Grief: New Directions, Challenges, and Strategies for Practice* (Champaign, Illinois: Research Press, 2002).

Viktor E. Frankl, *Man's Search for Meaning* (Boston: Beacon Press, 2014).

Pam Heaney, *Coming to Grief: A Survival Guide to Grief and Loss* (Dunedin: Longacre Press, 2002).

Lucy Hone, *What Abi Taught Us* (Auckland: Allen & Unwin, 2016).

Also published as Lucy Hone, *Resilient Grieving* (Auckland: Allen and Unwin, 2017).

Melissa M. Kelley, *Grief: Contemporary Theory and the Practice of Ministry* (Minneapolis: Fortress Press, 2010).

C. S. Lewis, *A Grief Observed* (London: Faber and Faber, 1961).

Richard Lischer, *Stations of the Heart: Parting with a Son* (New York: Vintage Books, 2013).

Henri J. M. Nouwen, *Out of Solitude: Three Meditations on the Christian Life* (Notre Dame, IN: Ave Maria Press, 1976.

Stephen Oliver (ed.), *Inside Grief,* (London: SPCK, 2013).

Colin Murray Parkes and Holly G. Prigerson, *Bereavement: Studies of Grief in Adult Life* (4th ed.) (London: Penguin Books, 2010).

Beth Allen Slevcove, *Broken Hallelujahs – Learning to Grieve the Big and Small Losses of Life* (Downers Grove, Illinois: IVP Books, 2016).

Hilary Smith, *Grief's Shadowed Path: Poems of Loss and Healing* (Napier: EVBooks, 2017).

Penelope Wilcock, *Spiritual Care of Dying and Bereaved People* (Abingdon: The Bible Reading Fellowship, 2013).

Caleb Wilde, *Confessions of a Funeral Director: How the Business of Death Saved My Life* (New York: Harper Collins, 2017).

Nicholas Wolterstorff, *Lament for a Son* (Grand Rapids, Michigan: Wm. B Eerdmans Publishing Co., 1987).

William J. Worden, *Grief Counselling and Grief Therapy: A Handbook for the Mental Health Practitioner*, 4th Ed. (New York: Springer Publishing, 2009).

Index

A

Abortion 56
Abuse 59
Acknowledging loss 29
Addiction 30
Adoption 51
  adoptees, identity and heritage 52
  adoptive parents 54
  birth parent 52
Alzheimer's disease, grieving for a person with 29
Anger
  and blame 172
  expression of 93
Attachment
  theory 126
  to a person or possession 124

B

Brain injury 30
Buried grief, dangers of 22

C

Capacity to grieve 26
Change
  and transition 62
  process of 200
Childlessness 49
Children and grandchildren
  becoming independent adults 64
Christian
  hope 208
  spirituality 10
Clichés
  avoiding 111
  religious 145
Closure (an unhelpful term) 77
Companioning Model of Bereavement Caregiving 119
Continuing bond with the dead 75

D

Dementia, grieving for a person with 29
Denial of grief 15
Depression 98
Disability
  grieving for yourself 34
  grieving the death of a person with 33
Disenfranchised grief 24, 60
Divorce 35
  affect on children 36
  judgement by others 37
  unrecognised grief 38

E

Easter Day 180
Embracing our grief 17
Experiences of grief
  behavioural reactions 97
  cognitive reactions 95
  different for differing losses 87
  emotional reactions to grief 91
  in our body 89
  isolation 86
  loneliness 94
  losing your memories of a person 29
  meaninglessness 198
  messy grief 69
  physical reactions to grief 90
  resilience 105
  significant loss
    affects of 85
  sufferer, grieving for oneself 30
  survival mode 67
  taking time off 71

F

Faith 99
  and grief 176
  changes and challenges to 178
  community 17
Finding meaning after loss 194
Former spouse or partner 40
Foster care 51
Frankl, Viktor 14
Funerals
  mourning the death of a loved one 144
Future, loss of 32

G

Gender and grief 81
God
  and our Grief 129
  encountering 155
  euphemisms and 139
  how our image of affects our grieving 138
  questions to about our loss 173
  suffering love of 134
  vulnerability of 132
  waiting in the darkness with 180
Good Friday 180
Gratitude 81
Grief
  ambush by 73
  as a journey 16
  as a spiral 70
  changes over time 72
  deceased person considered unworthy of 26
  distractions from 71
  pain of, responding to 186
  patterns of 81
  recognition of
    by others 88
    by the family of an older person 28
  the right to grieve 24
  unique to each person 65
  universal experience of 10
Guilt
  irrational 92
  rational 92

H

Helping someone who is grieving 107
  insensitive responses 55
  listening 108
  non-judgmental care 57
  speaking about our pain 171
  talk about the loss 113
  unhelpful questions 115
Holy Saturday 180
Hope energing after loss 205

I

Infertility 47

L

Lament 145
  and the church 158
Lewis, C. S. 13
Loss
  natural responses to 16
  of a companion animal or pet 41
    rituals for 43
  of a friend or colleague 40
  of a horse 42
  of employment, as source of identity 59
  of identity 101
  of opportunities and experiences 34
  of sexual intimacy 98
  types of 20
Love and grief 123

Index

M

Meaninglessness 203
Medical termination 56
Miscarriage 54
Mourning
  Jewish rituals of 165
  Sitting Shiva 165

P

Possessions, damage to or theft of 44
Professional intervention 104
Psalms, The
  and darkness 155
  of lament 147
  validating our experience of grief 150

R

Reconstructing meaning in our life 196
Redundancy 58
Relationships
  being sustained by 117
  ending of 36
  relational identity 102
  romantic, ending of 38
  unrecognised 39
Resurrection 143, 183

S

School fire 45
Search for meaning after loss 194
Self-disenfranchisement 26
Shock 96
Silence, tears and empathy 120
Spirituality 99
Stages of Grief model unhelpful 67
Stillbirth 55
Subsequent losses, chain of 47

U

Unemployment 57
Use of words in this book
  Bereavement 12
  Euphemisms and God 12
  Grief 12
  Loss 12
  Mourning 12

W

Wolterstorff, Nicholas 13

Also by Alister G. Hendery
from Philip Garside Publishing Ltd

Earthed in Hope:
Dying, Death and Funerals – A Pakeha Anglican Perspective.
2014 (Print and eBooks)

Earthed in Hope will enrich the funeral ministry both of those in the Anglican tradition and also those from other Churches. It is a valuable resource for funeral celebrants, counsellors and anyone supporting the bereaved and dying. Hendery reflects on and responds to spiritual, theological, liturgical, pastoral and cultural questions, and offers practical suggestions and insights that will be helpful to those involved in taking funerals and caring for the bereaved and the dying.

Praise for Earthed in Hope

"…For those concerned with funeral ministry there is much in this book that will repay careful reflection: how God and Christian hope are presented, the avoidance of euphemisms and idealistic eulogies, ritual at and after the funeral, funerals following suicide, funerals of children and children at funerals. Hendery states: 'We need to be able to look death in the face and be willing to wrestle with the theological, spiritual and emotional demands that this takes.' *Earthed in Hope* offers significant help for those who are serious about doing this."
Rev John Meredith, Touchstone – June 2015

www.ingramcontent.com/pod-product-compliance
Lightning Source LLC
Chambersburg PA
CBHW072001070526
44583CB00015B/1283